The Ideology of Hatred

The Ideology of Hatred

The Psychic Power of Discourse

Niza Yanay

FORDHAM UNIVERSITY PRESS

NEW YORK 2013

Fordham University Press has no responsibility for the persistence or accuracy of URLs for external or third-party Internet
websites referred to in this publication and does not guarantee
that any content on such websites is, or will remain, accurate or
appropriate.

Fordham University Press also publishes its books in a variety of
electronic formats. Some content that appears in print may not
be available in electronic books.

Library of Congress Cataloging-in-Publication Data is available
from the publisher.

Printed in the United States of America

15 14 13   5 4 3 2 1

First edition

CONTENTS

The movement in circular fashion from the individual subject to society is self-evident to me. Psychology and sociology, as I see them, are not two different modes of perception, not even two points of view. The psyche and the social always operate in tandem and form who we are as subjects and who we are as a society (whether we think of ourselves as singular or plural). The psyche cannot be conceived outside the bounds of language, and society, likewise, cannot be understood without taking into account the ways in which we as individuals use language, explicitly or implicitly, expressed or repressed. True, this double image of self and society cannot simply be taken for granted without attending to the paradoxes and theoretical difficulties that such movement entails. Yet what image of society can we form without the subject who speaks (and interacts)? And what subject is free from the power of society and interpellation, able to resist or conform fully to the law of society? And what are the subtexts—the anxieties—of language that constitute the unconscious? These social anxieties (individual and collective) as well as feared desires form the space through which the social, the political, and the psychical speak together in a conundrum.

Take violence, for example. Violence, I argue, must not be seen merely as a behavior, attitude, or emotion, aspects that define violence in most studies. Whether violence is a behavior, an attitude, or an emotion, it also indicates that "something" forbidden or unutterable demands satisfaction or fulfillment. Something has been erased but not lost. I am not saying that the function of violence is to simply create relief through expression, but rather that something unseen and unconscious demands fulfillment and satisfaction and that this something plays an intimate part in most atrociously violent moments in history. Indeed, this something has to be given a theoretical space if we aim to cultivate nonviolent practices and interactions. What are these unutterable demands that ask for satisfaction? What are the ways in which these demands speak? What are the anxieties and fears that, when expressed, cause others hurt and suffering?

Attempting to confront the abyss of hatred around me, and sensing and fearing the hatred in myself as well, I set out to write this book. I knew from the start that hatred per se is not what puzzles me. Rather, I long to see clearly what hatred comes to hide: the forces that endow representations of hatred with their power of signification.

First, however, I needed to confront the question of pleasure: my own pleasure in writing about hatred. How can I write with pleasure on hatred? What does it mean to write on hatred with pleasure? Can one attest to truth without writing with pleasure? Will my words be recognizable by others if I do not derive pleasure in writing? These questions led me back to Freud's method of understanding culture and society, and drove me to problematize collective hatred through my own experiences and relations of love and hate. I suspected that if I theorized my own fears of hatred that initially impelled this inquiry as well as the defenses that protect my love, as a Jew and an Israeli I might be able to better understand the identiterian hatred that I see between religious, ethnic, and national groups that live in close proximity. Thus writing on hatred from the place of my fears turned out to be a struggle of writing with pleasure—and this conscious struggle has turned out to be a particularly productive way to write the unconscious into a theory and social critique of hatred.

Precisely for this reason, I want to say a few words about what I learned from my father. In Chapter 4 I write a brief vignette that recalls a conversation with my father, who has always declared his resistance to hate, his refusal to give the Germans the pleasure of hating them. I grew up wondering how a person like my father, who survived Auschwitz, Buchenwald, and Teresienstadt, could love Man and believe in the future of humanity. I wonder how he, a secular person who survived the Shoah, could sustain his trust in the goodness of Man. Where did he find the power to resist hate and hope for a just, nonviolent, and democratic society in Israel/Palestine, his new homeland? I do not raise these questions now as a general existential puzzle. These questions arise from my own historical embeddedness, from memories of not being allowed and not allowing myself to ride in German-made cars like Volkswagen or to buy any product made in Germany. My father refused monetary compensation from the German government and refused to forgive Germans and Germany. Refusing to forgive yet refusing to hate? What does this mean? What does this say? How can this be? Somehow I know (but how?) that my fear of hatred and my father's refusal to forgive are connected. But I also know that without the concept of the unconscious (individual and social), his refusal to hate and forgive concomitantly would still not have made sense to me.

After the failure of the Oslo Accords, and as I was struggling to keep my faith in a possible future peace, I found my father's refusal to hate the Germans and the paradox of forgiveness the focal points from which I could begin thinking about national hatred. It was from this place that I could ask what hatred wants. What is it—through hatred—that must be denied or protected? What makes hatred for some necessary, legitimate, and a righteous expression in language? Do refusing to hate and loving to hate signify similar, even if contrasting, anxieties? These are some of the questions that I explore here by underscoring the psychic mechanisms and obstacles that form and represent national discourse and the ideology of hatred.

Finally, solutions often seem to be simple in intractable conflicts like the Israeli-Palestinian conflict. One needs, however, to ask why the two sides cannot come forward, declare friendship, and forgive each other, stop seeking justice, and begin living together in a shared land. Why is it impossible? What does this gap between possibility and impossibility signify, producing repetitive discourses of rejection, segregation, control, and oppression?

As I ask these questions, I hope it will be clear that this book is not meant to be polemical. I do not come to debate others. My main goal is to provide a critique of hatred that focuses on the relations between the unconscious and state politics, between imaginary fears and technologies of control. I rely on scholarly works and I do not reject others' explanations or different ways of seeing; I do not claim to fully know how hatred works, what it means, or what it wants. It is naïve to think that we can understand what hatred *is* or explain why people and groups hate. I do hope, however, to suggest different ways to think about utterances and practices of hatred: to suggest ways to theorize the discourse of hatred and thus contribute to an alternative discourse of friendship.

Writing the book was a long process. I started working on the meaning of hatred long before 9/11 but stopped right after losing my intellectual compass and sense of direction. After 9/11 I felt that something had changed globally, that a new discourse of hatred had entered politics in many Western democratic states. I resumed the work on hatred in 2008–9 when I became a member of the Institute for Advanced Study at Princeton. That year gave me the opportunity to return to the project and to move from a phenomenological critique to a psychoanalytic and deconstructive one.

I am thankful to many people at the institute; members and visitors, staff and faculty. First and foremost I want to thank Joan Scott, who generously offered her critique and suggestions. I also want to thank a small group of colleagues who formed what we jokingly called the "non-normative" group, a takeoff on the theme of the year: Social Norms and Cooperation. They are Jessica Cattelino, Aurelian Craiutu, Souad Eddouada, Richard Shweder, Danielle Allen, and Catherine Ross. Linda Garat and Donne Petito gave me friendly and efficient administrative guidance and assistance. Participating in the reading group on Sociology and Psychoanalysis in New York City during 2008–9 was a unique experience. I thank their members and particularly Catherine Silver for their important comments and for many good and productive discussions on the contested relations between sociology and psychoanalysis, past and present. Many women friends dear to me gave me invaluable emotional and intellectual support: Michal Aviad, Nitza Berkovitch, Janet Burstein, Susan Gubar, Talma Hendler, Sara Moray, and Reli de Vries. My friend Neve Gordon was like a lighthouse in the dark seas of writing. Catherine Rottenberg, my friend and kindred spirit, spent many hours of reading. Her comments and suggestions proved to me once again the pleasures of dialogue in the midst of inner chaos and self-doubt. Under the influence of Judith Butler's philosophical and political writings, I maneuvered my own voice. I thank her for her support and friendship. Great appreciation goes to the editorial team at Fordham University Press, they are Helen Tartar and Thomas Lay; at Westchester Publishing Services, Ellen Lohman and Michael Haggett. Finally, Yinon Cohen and Anna Cohen-Yanay; without them my life could not be whole. I dedicate the book to them.

The Ideology of Hatred

Introduction

Years before 9/11, living and working in Israel, I was perplexed by the diverse and mostly invisible workings of the word "hatred" and its place in national rhetoric and politics. When in 1989 I accidentally came upon about 400 letters of hate mail written by Jewish fundamentalists and sent to members of the Jewish political Knesset (the Israeli parliament) from Ratz (the party for citizens' rights), I began asking questions about the meaning and operation of hatred as a political force.[1] Much of my earlier research was based on empirical studies in Israel, which focused on the analysis of hate relations among Jews (secular and religious) and between Jews and Palestinians.[2] As a result of these studies I came to the conclusion that the concept of hatred is always an ambivalent mode of knowledge that holds at least two contradictory and opposite aims at once: the need for contact, dependency, inclusion, and proximity and the need for separation, differentiation, exclusion, and distance.[3]

However, after 9/11 my inquiry changed. It became clear that the production of the word "hatred" can no longer be viewed as a mere by-product of nationalism, racism, anti-Semitism, prejudice, or other evils and that questions of meaning will not lead me far enough in understanding how hatred operates ambivalently or what makes hatred so repulsive and pleasurable, outrageous and human simultaneously. Hence, this book is not a tour de force of the meaning of hatred or its various effects. Rather, expanding on my previous work, my aim is to show how invisible mechanisms of power operate when the word "hatred" is used as a defense strategy in a national and political context. The concept of hatred, of course, cannot be separated from history, language, and questions of identity. But I would further claim that first and foremost the understanding of hatred cannot ignore relations of power and its various uses and misuses. The 9/11 drama was certainly a critical event which has changed the concept of hatred from a psychological and emotional diagnostic term into a political public discourse. And this shift of status and meaning has convinced me that hatred must be retheorized primarily as an ideology of power and control.

After 9/11, the word "hatred" began to be used not only by the Bush administration but also by the media and politicians all over the democratic Western globe as a tactical and ideological word. Hatred became a political concept to signify danger, insecurity, and the need for control. The word became a discursive instrument of legal, social, and military practices. The Bush administration manipulated the use of hatred (particularly hatred directed toward America, capitalism, and the Western world) as a rhetorical trope to create legitimacy for its governmental policies and practices, its declaration of state emergency, and its active management of suspicion; for racial profiling; and for the military attack on Iraq. In the face of Bush's new dichotomy between those who hate and those who are the targets of irrational hatred, new questions about the relationship between politics and hatred must be asked.

To begin with, we must see hatred within regimes of unequal power relations. True, hatred is an embraced violence; the stronger and longer two rivalries fight, the stronger the embrace becomes. Yet it is never an equal embrace. Hatred *is* power but never an equal one. Many studies look at the practice of hatred as an exchange of emotional revenge and underscore the reciprocal relations of hatred[4]—"We hate them because they hate us." Yet hatred looked at from the perspective of unequal power relations, between marked and unmarked subjects, between the colonized and the colonizers, the ruled and the rulers, must be narrated at least twice: once through the site of resistance and once through the site of sovereign control, once as a force used by the oppressed and once as a force used by the oppressor.[5] Nonetheless, recent (academic and popular) writings on violence and hatred focus on the violence of the ruled, of the colonized, or of the oppressed other. That is not necessarily because the violence of the oppressed is more visible, but because state violence is often masked by "narcotic" terminologies of peace, order, and security. Most people consider "suicide bombing" an act of hate.[6] Fewer would see an air strike on populated areas as a hate crime, particularly when it is authorized by legal (Western) governments in the name of keeping world security, order, and democracy. The attempt to understand the hatred against America, Israel, and the West in many writings on hatred is a good example of this narcissistic tendency.[7] Over time it also became clear that in the name of democracy-building and operations of goodwill (humanitarian aid, peace talks, etc.), new frontiers of hatred were being opened: within the rhetoric of necessity, that is, necessary war (liberating and democratizing the other) in tandem with the rhetoric of security and peace (with those who do not hate). This trajectory, the production of hatred as an ideology of necessity, democracy, and peace raises difficult questions of misrecognition, veiled desires, and symptomatic significations—all of which are underrepresented in language and theory.

Therefore, two different forms of hatred need to be distinguished: hatred as a response to oppression and hatred as a structure of an ideology. Indeed, both forms signify power, yet in different ways, potency and politics. While reacting to power with hatred gives power, it remains the power of the meek, a denounced, criticized, and unaccepted power. In contrast, hatred producing ideology, hatred veiled in semantics of necessity (or responsibility for the nation) gives legal and political legitimacy to hatred. We must remember that these two forms of hatred are contingent on each other and connected in various contradictory and unforeseen ways in which both the oppressed and the oppressor are intertwined and respond to each other and to the conditions of their relations. On both sides, hatred exists in response. And yet the subject of oppression *reacts* to oppression, the sovereign to its own fears. Oppressive control necessitates an ideology of hatred, a legitimacy of violence. The task is therefore to understand the ideology of hatred as a regime of control, and not the subjects who respond to it. The task is to study the invisible mechanisms and the phantasmatic anxieties that constitute the other as an object of hate. Of course, not every conflict or competition breeds hatred. There are many social and political conflicts within democratic societies that arouse feelings of antagonism but do not engender discourses of hatred. Having said this, it is therefore not enough to focus on manifest violence; we must pay attention to the difference between the responses *to* power and the reactions *of* power.

There is not much to say about the hatred of the oppressed mostly because there is not much theoretical wonder to it. I will only say that throughout history, domination has been hated and resisted by oppressed people who struggled and rebelled, in different ways and by different means, against humiliation, discrimination, and conditions of servitude. It is therefore often more surprising when people do not rebel than when they do, or more puzzling when oppressed people do not hate than when they do. Most of us, perhaps on the basis of childhood memories, would admit resenting forced limitations, disciplinary orders, or control against our will. It is not hard to imagine how resentment against occupation, colonization, and exclusion takes the form of hatred and how this hatred becomes projected onto those in power, the privileged who, in the eyes of the oppressed, are responsible for their exploitation and the discrimination against them. Similarly, poverty, imprisonment, hunger, unemployment, humiliation, and loss become fertile grounds for feelings of hatred.

Not as obvious and more difficult to understand or theorize is the hatred of people who own "everything" and lack "nothing," that is, those in power who control the imaginary and the material resources of the nation. Think for a moment: why would a young adolescent girl in Israel, one who leads a comfortable life and has never interacted face to face with Palestinians, speak with vehement personal hatred against the Palestinians and Arabs in general? Why do so many Jewish Israelis, young and old, who have never been physically hurt by Palestinians admit to feeling intense hatred against them?[8] Why do so many Israeli leaders, in and outside the parliament, speak with such hatred against the Palestinians? And even more disturbing is the fact that many young children imagine the Palestinians as evil.[9] Responses such as "Because there is a real danger," "What about terrorism?" or the positivist logic "Because they hate us" come inevitably and automatically to our mind, and this is precisely because the power of the state (or state ideology) enables it to veil its fears through a rhetoric of violence and counterthreat to which we respond and hail at least to an extent until automaticity is refuted by critique.

In most cases of open political conflict between the ruled and the ruler, there is a struggle over who the real victim is and who has the right to hate. This tacit moral and political rivalry between the ruled and the ruler has been already stated.[10] The point I want to make is that hatred enhances an already inevitable *bond* between these two unequal yet not dichotomous sides of rival power. The understanding of hatred as a site of power relations underscores interiority and exteriority, desires and fears, intimacy and anxiety, approaching and avoiding the friend and enemy and dependencies between victims and victimizers in an unequal way. The discourse of hatred is contingent on these contradictions of intimacy and fear, proximity and distance, attachment and difference. On the one hand, the discourse of hatred produces separation and estrangement; on the other hand, the ideology of hatred mostly (but not singularly) hides that which cannot be thought in the field of the other, that threatening intimacy which must be disavowed and fought against. For the purpose of theory, the term "ideology of hatred" signifies the return of the repressed or the symptomatization of desire in the sphere of the social and the national. More specifically it claims the unthought-of dependency, or disavowed similarity, and proximity in the field of the other.

The dependency between the ruled and the ruler does not imply that their hatred is common or has an equal status or that these two modalities of hatred work similarly and engender a similar theoretical challenge.[11] It does indicate, however, that groups and people in relations of hatred are often tied together through desires that they refuse to admit.[12] It also indicates that these unconscious desires operate with intensity within (national, racial, or cultural and religious) discourse.

Most sociologists and political thinkers have ignored the place of the psyche in studies of war and peace. Postcolonial critique, however, suggests that the psyche and the political are not separate territories, that they operate within one site through different mechanisms, technologies and modes of representations and share a common discursive field through different forms of speech and visibility. Bhabha, Butler, Žižek, and Derrida, to name just the main few philosophers who are influential on my own writing, interweave the political and the hidden and absent in their understanding of the political. Each of them in different ways articulates how that which is said hides the unsaid and the disavowed and how that which is visible veils the hidden and the unrepresented, the necessary and impossible. Following this frame of thought, the question I wish to pursue and circle is not what hatred is, but *what does hatred want.*

Hence, the question of wants, desire, and pleasure stands in the heart of my inquiry of conflict relations and the ideology of hatred. I agree with Guattari that hatred lies everywhere,[13] and yet there is nothing that can be said about hatred that will be accurate under all circumstances and in all conflicts. At the same time, the social construction of hatred is not specific to any one particular conflict, but rather to specific conditions of power at a specific historical juncture. In this sense, I chose to be eclectic in my approach rather than to focus on one specific and singular conflict. Behind the words and thoughts presented in this book, readers will obviously discern the specter of the Jewish-Palestinian conflict—and this is only because this conflict constitutes *my* fears and hopes. It is not the most typical conflict (if there is one), but it is also not an atypical one. The cases of the former Yugoslavia, Rwanda, Armenia, Ireland, Darfur, India, Spain, and so forth are only a few possible examples of political or national conflicts in which groups living in proximity and intimacy of sorts (which I further articulate in Chapter 3) are bound together by hatred.

The conditions of closeness and proximity, I argue, form a sphere of *absence* (a surplus of desire) that I wish to map out in order to understand how neighboring groups, or people who are brought into our lives by circumstances, become the hated enemy; how intimacy and desire become a living, vital category in politics.[14] When President Habyarimana of Rwanda gave his famous speeches between 1973 and 1994, he explicitly attacked the Tutsi as counterrevolutionary bourgeoisie traitors. At the same time, he referred to them as brothers.[15] The use of intimate, familial language to characterize the other within as a traitor and enemy is a common practice in many ideologies of hatred. For example, in "street speech" within Zionist ideology, the Palestinians are often derogatively referred to as "our cousins."[16] What can be understood from such language, the calling of the enemy by familiar (familial) pronouns of intimacy? What does it mean to misrecognize what language reveals? And what effects do unthought desires have on war and peace?

One does not need to hate or feel hatred in order to be evil, intentionally hurt others, or even kill. Neither rage nor war that results in atrocious violence is necessarily a direct indicator of hatred. There are, of course, other options, speculations, possibilities. Love, for example. Why do we assume that Muhamad Atta was driven by hate? Why do we believe that hatred speaks of hatred alone? Or speaks only to hatred and to it alone?[17] Clearly, the twenty-first century is the age of hatred. Neither the Great War nor World War II made hatred its celebratory nodal concept. Of course, hate has appeared on the stage of history, but only as a passing word, an epiphenomenon of totalitarianism, prejudice, anti-Semitism, and racism, never as an ideology in itself. The place of hatred in racism or anti-Semitism was clearly recognized, but only as a statement or a recognized by-product of ideology, not a discourse in itself that became today a category, a label attached to signify different conflicts. We are in the age of hatred not because there is more hatred or violence in the world; wars, atrocities, and killing have always been part of the record of communities and societies: from Cain and Abel to the Palestinian camps, from Genghis Khan to modern genocides. This is also not to say that violence is necessarily part of human nature, but rather that violence became natural to humans and to their diverse societies, however organized and structured. So what has changed? After 9/11, for the first time, we can say that hatred has become a legitimized discourse in the form of governmental-state politics. The event of 9/11 marks a discursive turn; it has become a *point de capiton*, a nodal point, a privileged signifier "that fixes the meaning of a signifying chain" generally pointing at hatred.[18]

Following 9/11, hatred has become a discourse of *danger* in and of itself, an apparatus of rhetorical control producing new enemies and new rhetorical politics of proximities.[19] The word "hatred" has become a signifier of a new condition, a useful category for the purpose of legitimizing forms of biopolitics, emergency states, and war. In fact, the rhetoric of hatred has "invaded" the public domain, where it is seen no longer as a personal feeling, but as a category determining social and political relations. The concept of hatred, once irrelevant to the study of politics, began circulating in speeches, writings, and public discussions as the new object of fear. The word "hate" began operating as a social force of manipulation and mobilization. Hatred and danger have thus become a construction that is synonymous with necessary action against forces of difference.

In the name of protecting the world's security, peace, and democracy, the Bush administration reinscribed territorial and emotional maps of exclusion and belonging. Just think of the repeated, obsessive notices in the New York City subways: "If you see something, say something." Such an utterance not only speaks of suspicious objects but also creates relational mistrust that paradoxically bonds people together through a fearful gaze, suspicion and prejudice through the very act of atomization and othering. Terms such as "racial hatred" (rather than racism), "religious hate," "hate conflicts," "national hatred," "hating strangers," and "hate crimes" circulate in the media and public announcements and are understood to constitute a fundamental reality. Once considered one emotion among many others, hatred is now the new form of the "uncanny." The use of hatred is so pervasively dominant—"the new popular"—that old and new violent struggles for autonomy, national conflicts, and aspirations for self-determination of colonized and postcolonized peoples fighting through unconventional techniques such as suicide bombing and guerilla operations are now being reformulated as hate politics.[20]

Yet this book is not a linguistic inquiry. I do not wish to demonstrate, characterize, or describe the various faces of hatred. Many have already done so from different academic and nonacademic perspectives. Rather, my aim is to investigate the politics of hatred that is absent from the discourse and yet part of its very constitution. I argue that in order to understand this politics, we need to uncover the invisible mechanisms that operate within the political, which are not spoken yet determine the lives of people around the globe. Such an inquiry presupposes certain territorial, economic, and technological circumstances, a certain reality (such as labor migration, global economic production, technological innovations of control and surveillance, and so on) that takes part in the production of the surplus of the unspoken. But these circumstances are not the primary focus of my critique. Rather, my aim is to bring into focus the libidinal processes working behind the scenes within discourse, to provide a critique of the libidinal unconscious in the social field built through a history of social, national, ethnic, and religious group relations, which Deleuze calls the "subjectivity" of the political that goes beyond the subject as a collective desire.[21] How then do proximities and distances, similarities and differences, pleasures and anxieties come to constitute the politics of hatred? What is the ideology of hatred that operates as a regime of control and produces the new discourse of violence?

My starting point is the recognition that hate today is "involved in the very negotiation of boundaries between selves and others, and between communities, where 'others' are brought into the sphere of my or our existence as a threat."[22] This definition, which attempts to avoid framing power relations in psychological terms or reifying institutions, emphasizes the politics of hatred that communities bring into their daily life as a felt "invasion" of others and as a discourse of threat. It suggests that hate relations are a form of construction that dictates harsh negotiations of boundaries and identities, but first and foremost it emphasizes the active unconscious force of affective categorizations and its emotional politics. With linguistic signifiers such as the "clash of civilizations," "Muslim terrorism," or "axis of evil," a split language, between those who are dangerous and threatening and those who must fight against evil, is brought into "our" life. The split between those who ought to be hated (who are not loyal, the rebels, the different) and those in power who have the moral and political legitimacy to hate forms at the same time a rhetoric that condemns hatred and sees it as necessary at once. If, for example, a politics of suspicion and exclusion is perceived as necessary, hatred then becomes ostensibly transparent.

By calling attention to the split language of hatred, I do not claim to support one regime of truth over another or justify certain methods of violence and condemn others. All modes of killing are crimes; all victims, regardless of their side, Tutsi or Hutu, Serbs or Croats, Africans or Muslims, should receive our support and help. But this is not the point. No ideology (economic, national, or religious) can wear the ribbon of pureness on its flag. I am merely pointing to the connection between sovereign power and the rhetoric of hatred, to the bifurcated discourse of legitimate and illegitimate hatred, and to the people who are stigmatized as haters, and therefore enemies in contrast to those who "only" hate the haters.

I therefore do not see the intellectual and political productivity in a dictionary definition of hatred. Like love, there are many visible and

invisible modes of knowing and unknowing hatred. Providing a definition will only produce new opaqueness and misrecognitions. I can only
say that I use the word "hatred" not as one concept, but a concept split by
power. At the same time, regardless of one's power, hatred presents a
paradox: the more we strive to separate ourselves from the (hated) other,
the more strongly we become attached to him or her. The more determined we are to destroy the other, the more dependent on him or her we
become. This paradox, which operates within the discourse of hatred as
an *invisible structure of attachment*, whether recognized or unrecognized,
is the focus of the book.[23]

This is not a study of just any hatred. I specifically focus on relations
that take the form of impossibility, on attachments that are prohibited and
unthinkable. Particularly, I discuss those fantasies against hated others
seen through the blind spot of desire. I propose that the ideology of hatred
(racism, anti-Semitism, Islamophobia, and so on) signifies areas of attachments and dependencies that are necessary yet impossible and unthinkable.
Or put differently, the ideology of hatred marks the unsignified spoken in
discourse. If, as Butler says, prejudice "neither begins nor ends with the subject who speaks and acts,"[24] in what follows, I attempt to understand how
that power of neither/nor operates, what the tacit mechanisms are through
which the political becomes a symptom of discourse. Such a task focuses
primarily on the system and its apparatuses that produce hate discourse
rather than on specific subjects who speak and act even when the boundaries are not clear cut.

Primo Levi once said: "[But] there is no rationality in the Nazi hatred; it
is a hate that is not in us; it is outside man, it is a poison fruit sprung from
the deadly trunk of Fascism, but it is outside and beyond Fascism itself. We
cannot understand it, but we can and must understand from where it
springs, and must be on our guard."[25] Hatred is *not in us*, says Levi, but has
the power to seduce us, to haunt us through the sovereignty of "the beyond
ideology of ideology," that surplus passion and desire beyond the language
of ideology. If it is not in us and, moreover, it is beyond ideology, where is
the "place" of hatred? Does hatred have a place, a marked topography? Is
this only Levi's way of saying that hatred resists understanding and that its
motives, meaning, and wants are never fully comprehensible? Is hatred a
transgressive territory beyond proclamations and boundaries? Or are "not

in us" and "beyond ideology" perhaps the topology of the surplus or the Real in Lacan's language, that excluded text that forms the tacit power of discourse—the unconscious of discourse? Levi demanded to know "from where it [hatred] springs," not in terms of the origin of hate, but in the sense of its "reason" and "logic." Yet at this point in time, after 9/11, what needs to be studied is not that which comes to be manifested in hatred—the logic or illogic of atrocities and barbarism—but rather the missing links of what hatred *wants* through discourse, the denied signifiers of which hatred is their effect and their symptom; silenced desires, signifiers of panic, and the "invisible archive" that constitutes the unconscious of hate discourses.

In the light of this split, I turn to explore aspects of the unconscious of discourse, or more specifically questions of desire; the desire of (but also to and for) the prohibited other. My question is directed at a reality that in Bataille's expression is an *inaccessible obscurity*. Particularly I explore the psychic mechanisms that constitute the discursive ruses that transform the unthinkable into a legitimized spoken language that is not itself, or what I term the collective unconscious (if there is one). In a climate of suspicion and political justification of state violence against outside and inside danger, academic scholarship has harnessed itself to answer "what is hatred."

I take a different course: focusing on the ways in which unconscious desires work hyperbolically in the service of political forces. It is not surprising, says Žižek, that Freud borrowed the quote "dare to move the underground!" from Virgil as a motto for *The Interpretation of Dreams*. To study the invisible, that which sovereign politics hides, it is necessary to bring into consciousness those "dark underground unthought thoughts," the knowledge that is disavowed from discourse, to recognize the absent language which raises obstacles every time a truce or peace accord is set in motion. Most of all, however, my work is indebted to Freud's *Totem and Taboo*. In *Totem and Taboo*, Freud inscribes the first guideposts to the internalization of guilt and its reparation through which social solidarity and bonding are established. Civilization opens with the murder of the father by his sons, the brothers, followed by a bond between them and the formation of a community of rival brothers committed to the dead sovereign father and his laws. One could argue with this narrative. Yet if we continue with this social psychological direction, can we ask what happened to guilt in the twenty-first century? Does hatred take the place of guilt? Do attachment and its disavowal become the key problems of ideology?[26]

Finally we come to the main question: what does hatred want? Hatred speaks from the place of enmity and abjection in a passionate way, forming its own discourse and politics. But hatred, we must note, speaks as a borderline language. Hatred speaks in one voice but with many hyperbolic sublanguages: the language of death and desire, exclusion and inclusion, detachment and attachment, and it always breaks out in the space between convention and the violation of the rules. It dominates societies through every institution and system, without exclusion, penetrating the entire discursive field whether one resists or submits to its passion. It is a mistake to believe that one can be free of hatred in a society that promotes an ideology of hatred, as much as one cannot transcend racism in a society with a tradition of racism. Although through critique and active resistance we can take responsibility for racism or avoid hate language, these conscious acts only indicate of resistance that hatred has not vanished from our psyche or from our habitual identifications. Albert Memmi wisely wrote that even the anti-occupation Frenchman in Algeria remained after all a colonialist who resists and practices colonialism at once. Yet we want to believe that there is a difference between those who justify hatred and those who fight against it not only as a state of mind but as a force of change.

It would be a mistake to assume that the ideology of hatred works exclusively through straightforward forms of speech or spectacles of violence. Often, what seems noble and humanitarian is part of the same narcissistic relations of production that signify prejudice and hatred. For example, one of the paradoxes of hatred can be demonstrated through the discourse of modern toleration. In *Regulating Aversion*, Wendy Brown contends that tolerance is a discourse of power that disguises aversion and hostility toward the other within. In the name of civility and peace, objects of tolerance are marked as undesirable. Hence tolerance, she argues, becomes an ideology of control and governance. The ideology of hatred can operate side by side and in tandem with humanitarian aid without any apparent contradiction, such as in the American initiative to build secular schools for girls in Pakistan and Afghanistan and in the Israeli provision of food and medical aid to Gaza in the midst of Israel's military attacks and destruction of civil life. Nonetheless, this rhizomatic topography of differentiated forces proceeds as a collective assemblage in transversal communication, forming together the map of state control. What I wish to stress is that when people take part in a system that denies its oppression and hatred of the other yet continues to disregard the life and well-being of the other as a regular political strategy—and that from time to time (particularly when the international community raises questions) allows a "corridor" of aid as a humanitarian spectacle—people (both individuals and collectives) come to believe that they are decent and righteous. In reality, "humanitarian corridors" are part of the continuation of war and violence in a language of *love full of hatred*. Again, I am not saying that humanitarian aid is unimportant. It does save lives under crisis. And sometimes that is the only form of help individuals can give to the other in situations of intractable conflicts. Sometimes it is the only way on the individual level to show resistance to war machines.[27] However, it is important to recognize and remember that humanitarian aid, like the liberal concept of toleration, together with the feelings of self-satisfaction and solace it brings to the social and political sphere is still part of the same system of war and hatred. To this denial and its defensive counterpart, a language of *hatred full of love*, to this *political unconscious* and its workings, I now turn.

What would love full of hatred (or hatred full of love) be if not the politics of the unconscious? Whether social fantasy or political economy, love full of hate and hate full of love depict concrete situations and relations that signify repressed desire, and a politics that hyperbolically controls the subject's desire of the other as well as the other's enmity and abjection. The prohibition of love of the other, at work within national loyalty and politics, a prohibition that functions as an imperative obligation to the tribal group, is perhaps the core paradoxical symptom of nationalism and its defenses; the prohibition already represents desire that must be disavowed. Following Deleuze, we could say that conflicts of love and hate, the blind discourse of nationalism, signify the unconscious of discourse itself. Otherwise it is hard to understand why conflicts, which are easily settled by territorial divides, compensations, security zones, and so forth, reoccur again and again without a *satisfying* (in the psychoanalytic sense) end, as if there is something else, a surplus, that the conflict and its politics are not telling us. One could always argue that the propagation and fixation of conflict are due to contradictory demands, to competition, or to a lack of trust and unfit communication, but what is mistrust if not a signified anxiety of love in hatred, attachment which the discourse of hatred comes to disguise as claims of "missed-trust"?

The political is structured as a language that hides its unconscious. As a language that is not named, a language of impossibility, it constitutes its own limits, holes, and respite. To depict the unconscious politics of hatred, its signified ideology, we must articulate the spectral appearances of hatred as both gaps (in language) and surplus (desire), mark and trace through each individual event but also systemically the way in which desire penetrates the social field of relations and disappears into the underground of words and actions. For that reason the situation "necessary and impossible" will form an important concept in my thesis on the ideology of hatred (see Chapter 3). It encapsulates the idea that relations of conflict, which are always also a form of proximity and intimacy, depict and deny the contingent relations between love and hate, the dependency between the rulers and the ruled through the somatization of the social. Specifically, the caesura between necessity and impossibility forms the politics of hatred and the unconscious of discourse.

I argue that the political unconscious operates as a psychic apparatus within discourse. It works as a system of renunciation and denial within national discourse in the service of that which is known and unknown, spoken and unspoken in the field of the other. The political unconscious produces tactics of detachment within a system of attachments, proximity, and dependencies and techniques of inclusions in the form of surveillance in order to manage that which is necessary and impossible. The psychology of the "possible impossible" maintains a safe divide between the enemy and friend, love and hate; it guards the psychic relations of necessity, which are always fundamentally threatening, outside conscious discourse. Desire has no law and yet national desire operates as law, constituting the double bind of politics and desire within discourse.[28] On the one hand the politics of violence denies the dependency between the ruler and the ruled, the enemy and friend. On the other hand the language of hatred, operating as a discursive defense, sustains the passion of desire alive under circumstances of its impossibility. Perhaps the most poignant understanding of the tragic, impossible, and necessary dependency between the rulers and the ruled is provided by Memmi's Hegelian portrait of the colonialist ruler.[29] Memmi portrays with great psychological precision the existential position of the colonialist, who on the one hand "wishes" to dismiss the colonial subject from thought, to imagine the colony without its natives, but who on the other hand "knows" that without its colonial subjects the colony has no meaning. This place of unrecognized conflict of dependency and hatred is precisely the lacuna where the legislative law and the law of desire coincide. It is Memmi's intimate understanding of the colonial state (but also Fanon's and Bhabha's) that sheds light on the invisible war (in tandem with its visible means) of the colonizer against the colonized and against his or her own desire, which produces hatred as both conscious and unconscious politics that must keep the colonized subject alive continuously facing the threat of catastrophe.[30] The means of oppression and humiliation are often clear, but the motivations are bounded through dark alleys of desire that produce the fetish power of hatred.

How can desire come into the relation of enmity and hatred, into relations of dependency between the ruler and the ruled that are the furthest possible antithesis to love, respect, and understanding? To understand this, we must view desire as a diabolical concept of life and death, the "little death" in Bataille's language of sin and eroticism, of that violence which stands in opposition to the incongruous other. "The Other is the locus in which [the subject] is situated . . . it is the field of that living being in which the subject has to appear," writes Lacan.[31] This is to say that the other governs "whatever may be made present of the subject," that the subject is realized within a contingent chain of significations, which are in the locus of the other and on which the subject depends for its own subjectivation. This "law" of subjectivation—the law of desire—presupposes the other to whom a need is addressed and a demand is made.

This general law, however, requires some historical specifications, particularly as questions in the field of politics. For example, who is the other from which a response is required? And what if the other, to whom desire is addressed, is also the enemy, the abject, and the hated other? That is to say, what are the connections between the violence of the passions and the violence of control?[32] Psychoanalysis tells us that "not to want to desire" and "to desire" are the same situation with different consequences. In national conflicts, the compliance of the ruled encourages the ruler to believe that he or she is loved and good; resistance disrupts the fantasy of love, and therefore love must be demanded. And so, through violent and disciplinary measures, love becomes regulated and controlled.[33] In the gap between obedience and resistance, love and hate are divided and blurred in a transgressive movement "destined for the abyss."[34] The language of conflict becomes a language of horror and violence but also of joy and desire of death that crosses the lines of divisions, distance, and separation, opening up a space that touches "absence itself."[35] There comes a time where the transgression unto death takes the form of destroying that which is impossibly loved (whether in politics or writing). This is the moment of genocide, the erotization of death and destruction.

The domination of hatred as a discourse of power emerges precisely from the gap between the *must* (the want) and the *horrific* (the forbidden), or the gap between the desire of the other and its unthinkable horror. But the discourse of hatred is not yet the moment of killing; the discourse of hatred anticipates indifference toward the other. When the killing starts, desire transforms into the ecstasy of murder, and indifference to the life of the other begins. The internal image of the other disappears and with it the "soul" of the killer. Hence, the discourse of hatred poses a paradox of desire: on the one hand the desire of the other is unthinkable, forbidden, and repressed. On the other hand it is precisely the desire of the other that the subject wants, must own, and must control to rule. These diabolic double movements—want and fear, ownership and the precariousness of life—bring relations of power to a heightened violence.

For example, in a dialogue group of Israeli Jewish and Arab students, Jewish Israelis obsessively kept on demanding, time and again, that the Arabs declare their loyalty toward and love of the state of Israel, but they would never, not for a moment, have believed or accepted such a declaration (I will demonstrate this process in Chapter 3).[36] I suppose that through their demand for love (yet never accepting it), the Jewish students created an illusory sphere of mastering desire, an imaginary control of the possible impossible. In this way they could own the pleasure of the other and reject their desire at once again and again, taking one step forward toward the other and two steps back, feeling dominant yet anxious, and never for a moment being aware that denied love is the problem and not hate. This process demonstrates the power of the unconscious in discourse and the way in which the psyche operates in the service of hegemonic national discourse.

Similarly, if we observe the kind of conflicts in the world today, and listen to the articulations given to the danger that states today face from within or from the outside, it is hard not to see the ambivalence of love and hate, similarity and difference, dependency and differentiation, separation and connectedness, exclusion and inclusion; these ambivalences surface, clash, and come together under the rhetoric of security and the need to protect democracy and freedom.

In the times of the Iliad, cruel wars were fought in the name of angry gods to spare and save their honor and pride. Modern nationalism and colonialism were driven by a desire for territorial expansion and domination over wealth. But since the twentieth century, wars and conflicts mainly exhibit fears of dependency and hybridity. How else can we comprehend Nazism, racism, anti-Semitism? It is no wonder that, according to historians, the twentieth century was the bloodiest century in history and the most violent. Certainly it is not simply a matter of advanced technology that has exacerbated modern destruction—the Hutu, for example, used machetes. I argue that the level and magnitude of aggression escalate with increasing repression of love, denial of attachments, and fears of dependency. In Israel, Lebanon, Rwanda, Burundi, Congo, Northern Ireland, Kashmir, France, Germany, and so forth, groups fight over unity, purity, and superiority, that is, over issues of proximity and dependency and the nature of living together separately.[37] The politics that underlies these ambivalent absent attachments is not necessarily visible to the eye of newspaper readers. It requires close attention to the underground operations within speech. In Chapter 3, I speak of the politics of idealization (the imaginary fantasy of the absent "good" other) and splitting (a caesura between the "good" and the "evil" other), which work in tandem and engender a discourse of hate as a metonymic opposite to fears of attachment. Through forces of idealization and splitting, repressions, denials, and misrecognition, that hidden mechanism of the political unconscious and the signifiers of dependency, similarity and attachment, enter the social field of speech and action yet subverted as a discourse of hatred. Love is displaced from one system of knowledge to another; from the conscious to the unconscious, from "them" to "us," and from recognition to misrecognition in speech.[38] Fears of dependency and proximity are subverted into legitimized violence and even deadly acts. In this age of multitude and postmodern nationalisms, could it be the case that peace has become even more threatening than war?[39]

My main point, then, is that the ideology of hatred today represents political forces that engender and determine the trajectories of rejected and foreclosed desire. It could be said that in some ways the disavowed desire of the other is the new political unconscious of postmodern wars (in contrast to, for example, eighteenth-century romantic colonialism and the paternalistic fascination with the other). And if so, is hatred ipso facto also the condition and possibility of love? Perhaps precisely because of the ambivalent tensions of interior/exterior, absent/present speech, the politics of hatred can change because the enemy is forever the lost friend. Prohibitions can be resisted, the unthought thought, and the other can be reconfigured as a neighbor and friend. This double movement between one form of political fantasy—annihilating the object of desire—and another form of political reimagination—unknotting the fear of the other—also produces the movement between the enemy and friend. My last chapter focuses on political friendship. Many speak of "permanent peace"—the "eternal peace"—as being the ultimate goal of reconciliation. But peace is not a theology. Peace is only a form of friendship, and friendship is not without conflicts or anger; yet it does contain within it recognized love and responsibility that can detour hatred.

The concept of the political unconscious suggests that the field of politics and the site of the unconscious overlap. Politics and the unconscious are two different regimes, but not two different territories. This understanding is particularly significant when we analyze the discourse of hatred as an ideology and apparatus of control. We must not overlook the forces of the invisible within the visible, the internal within the external, attachment within the terms of detachment, desire within prohibitions, and proximity within distance. As Freud discerned, love can swiftly change to hate (and vice versa) and the friend into an enemy (and vice versa). Some conflicts are intractable, are hard to change, and appear fixated. Yet if we listen carefully to the language of desire in the midst of conflict and war, if we trace its invisible hyperbolic movements and paradoxes, if we better understand the psychic territory with its contradictions and denials, we could fight the transgression of love to hatred to ignite the change from hatred to friendship. This change, as Freud remarked, can indeed come swiftly, because it is simply always possible. And Žižek reconfirms Freud's idea by further noting that "the politics of hate is sometimes the only proof that love can be rescued and survive."[40] Ambivalence is the force of history. And therefore the change from the impossible to the possible can be swift. It only requires the right moment in history and the right circumstances. We do not need to wait for the future to prove it. In fact, the possibility of transforming hatred to friendship is the raison d'être of this book.

Hatred and Its Vicissitudes

After the two world wars and the Holocaust, how is it possible that at the end of the twentieth century and beginning of the twenty-first century we have come to witness so much hatred toward the Other? Obviously, as Hardt and Negri have pointed out, globalization (the new politics of proximity and multitude) plays a prominent role.[1] Yet why do new world proximities produce so much threat and hatred? The idea that intimate "proximity" advances new forms of violence shows how little we know about the apparatus of hatred in local and global politics. Today, in an age of the multitude, the difficult task before us is not necessarily to explain national, ethnic, and religious hatred, but to theorize the new violence of proximity as the forces of understanding hatred.

Despite the enormous amount of studies on violence in general and racism, anti-Semitism, prejudice, bigotry, and homophobia in particular, the concept of hatred as ideology, that is, the symptom of the repressed in the field of the social and the political, is conceptually opaque and inadequately studied. Hatred is, of course, an emotional force, a strong, passionate force, but is it only an internal feeling? When hate occupies and dominates the public sphere, how does hatred become an apparatus of discourse and a political machine? How does hatred enter and affect politics? To answer these questions, we have to first understand the uses and misuses of the concept of hatred as an overt and covert language that constitutes thought, speech, and actions.

The most common misconception of hatred is the use of "rage" as a synonym for "hatred." In his treatise on hatred, Glucksmann, the French philosopher, consistently associates rage with hatred, and in this he is not unique. In their review of recent meanings of hatred, Royzman, McCauley, and Rozin conclude that personalized, generalized, or globalized anger has become a popular view of hatred.[2] However, when rage or strong anger is linked to hatred, it is often in the service of a particular ideological tie, linking the anger of the oppressed with hateful attitudes and emotions. A critical approach to power relations, inequality, and oppression has to question the tie between "rage" and "hatred" often used as two synonymous words with equal valance and connotative meaning. In unequal power relation of proximity and difference, the questions are, who has the power to use these words metonymically, and how does rage become stigmatized as hatred?

The important distinction that bell hooks advances between hatred and "killing rage" is worth noting. It opens a semiotic space for critique and raises consciousness not only to the cultural politics of emotions but also to the workings of hegemonic stigmatization and markings. Rightly bell hooks declares: "The rage of the oppressed is never the same as the rage of the privileged."[3] Minorities' anger against the conditions of oppression is not their "nature" and "character," but a strategy of the powerless to gain power. We must rearticulate rage from the point of view of the oppressed, she claims, precisely in order to fight hatred. Similarly, writing on her experiences in Algeria, Helene Cixous says: "I want to talk about hatred, in Algeria, about a certain quality of hatred that united us, a composite of *hope and despair* (my emphasis)."[4] Cixous draws attention to the hatred of the oppressed as "a certain quality" of subjectivation, close to what Wendy Brown defines as "wounded attachments"; a history of pain, resentment, and hope that constructs the subject. hooks advances the concept of "killing rage" in order to characterize that which is left within the control of the oppressed, the psychic "ammunition" of the colonized, and the power of refusal enabling the oppressed to defy hatred. In a powerful and personal narrative, hooks writes in *Killing Rage* about her humiliating experience of racism: "It was the sequences of racialized incidents involving black women that intensified my rage against the white man sitting next to me. I felt a 'killing rage.' I wanted to stab him softly, to shoot him with the gun I wished I had in my purse. And as I watched his pain, I would say to him tenderly 'racism hurts.' With no outlet, my rage turned to overwhelming grief and I began to weep, covering my face with my hands. . . . I leaned towards him with my legal pad and made sure he saw the title written in bold print: 'killing rage.'"[5]

Is this, that is, being in a rage, hatred? Killing rage for hooks is not only an experience—a feeling—but a fantasy of power. hooks, like Cixous or Toni Morrison, imagines hope for black people in her rage. "There is presence in anger," she cites Morrison's narrator in *The Bluest Eye;* "it is that presence, the assertion of subjectivity . . . that surfaces when the colonized express rage." Black rage is also the idiom that privileged whites defensively and stereotypically identify with black people's nature and with their own fear. But great rage, for hooks, is counterfactual to white hatred, which is also manifested as fear. True "racial hatred is real," she says, and "it is humanizing to be able to resist it with militant rage."[6] In contrast to white fear, black rage is a mode of resistance against black victimization, a struggle of liberation from white supremacy. Although rage, like hate, is a burning feeling, it is, unlike hatred, a constructive, healing, and transformative response to racism. Rage is a signifier of critical consciousness, an antidote to hatred, the kind of effect that characterizes politicized subjects. hooks admits: "Confronting my rage, witnessing the way it moved me to grow and change, I understood intimately that it had the potential not only to destroy but also to construct. Then and now I understand rage to be a necessary aspect of resistance and struggle. Rage can act as a catalyst inspiring courageous action."[7] On the one hand, rage reflects an ambivalent identification with difference and belonging, agency and social responsibility; but on the other hand, hooks theorizes black rage as a discourse of justice, a theory of rebellion and transformation. It is directed toward liberating the oppressed rather than destroying the oppressor; not that rage cannot become hatred, but the automatic association assuming a resemblance between rage and hatred is part of hegemonic ideology that misses the difference between political subjects and barbarism.

In the chapter "Wounded Attachments," Wendy Brown questions the political value of rage and its transformative powers.[8] Can the venting of injurious emotions such as pain and suffering activate liberatory practices or be the basis for a theory of freedom? Is it not just a therapeutic moment that at the same time also fixes "the identities of the injured and the injuring as social positions"?[9] Following Nietzsche's concept of *ressentiment*, Brown problematizes the painful feelings of the oppressed. How and in what way can wounded feelings re-signify the desire for justice and freedom? Brown poses two contradictory and unequal possibilities: on the one hand, resentment can be used as a self-righteous speech of injustice that morally legitimizes the revenge of the powerless. On the other hand, resentment signifies a language of desire for freedom, used and mobilized by politicized identities. While the first option assigns external blame, the second option transforms the conditions of oppression. Politicized identities produce a discourse of difference that subverts white, capitalist, middle-class, and masculine ideals and creates imaginary states of desire as the horizon for daily emancipative struggles and practices.

Indeed, feelings of pain, bitterness, resentment, and personal loss inform (yet do not cause) a killing rage. Killing rage, the way hooks and Morrison use it in their writings, accords with Brown's second option underscoring transformative processes, thus changing personal revenge to liberatory consciousness and action. hooks's distinction between the helpless internalization of victimization and the language of killing rage converses with Brown's differentiation between the politics of resentment and the emancipative project undertaken by politicized identities. Rage gives injury and humiliation what Brown calls an "alternative future." hooks's concept of "killing rage" (in contrast to pathological rage) speaks of a vision from the place of a subject who knows what he or she wants for the future. It stands against a racist, nationalist, or sexist culture and its social norms. When one embraces victimization, one surrenders to pathological hatred. For hooks, as for Brown, to surrender one's rage means to give up the future and hope. The rage of the oppressed is not about self-recovery (although it can be about that, too), but is primarily a signified desire for justice and social reform. Rage resists the relations of colonization (although it does not abolish its conditions) and hatred; it is a suturing practice between social and political subjectivity. True, colonized subjects hate their oppression.[10]

Yet hating oppression and promoting a discourse of hatred must not be confused.

hooks's Benjaminian logic and particularly her distinction between forms of violence (liberatory versus oppressive) may be problematic to those who view actions as well as concepts of violence (excluding self-defense) as illegitimate means of struggle.[11] But Walter Benjamin's moral and theological logic benefits the critique of hatred by shifting the focus from a natural and neutral perspective, which supports blaming the oppressed, to an understanding of the complexities of violence and the necessary distinctions between violence embedded in social institutions and the dominant language, and the structure of power and violent rage as a force of justice. Benjamin's critique of violence responds to legal reason and to the normalization of ideals by the law (itself a form of violence), which defines, for its own protection, all forms of violence, including at times acts intended to advance social change, as illegal. Benjamin's distinction between justice (the only criterion for deciding what form of violence is justified) and power points at the blindness of authorities to their own violent strategies. States often use the law to justify unjustified means (and ends) and outlaw justified forms of struggle, for example, civil protest. If all forms of violence are outlawed, he asks, how can people ever change the conditions of their oppression; how can they fight for their national, civil, or human rights? This debate, of course, is larger and more complex than I could possibly develop here. The point I wish to stress is that the politics of "hating oppression" and hatred as ideology, although interconnected realities, are two different concepts of justice.

Again, I am not saying that there are justified and unjustified forms of hatred. I do contend, however, that *objective hatred* (in response to oppression) and *ideological hatred* (in response to fear) are different discourses of power. The concept of hatred used in detachment from power and control, as in most psychological and social conceptualizations of hatred, legitimizes the use of state violence against the rage of the oppressed. The distinction (but not separation) between hating oppression and the ideology of hatred opens a new space of interrogation and critique; it raises a new series of questions in the domain of the political, particularly questions of desire (who wants what) and entitlement (who is allowed to enjoy freedom). By putting the emphasis on such conceptual differentiations, we can avoid giving state power a neutral meaning of truth. Think of colonized subjects, immigrant workers, religious minorities, people who work hard to integrate (not assimilate) into civil society, to prosper, to give their children a good education, gain respect, recognition . . . pleasure. Think of their rage at being marked as dangerous people only because of belonging to a group labeled stereotypically by the grammatical machine of the state. To understand the politics of hatred, we must remember these differences.

On another level, hatred as an apparatus of ideology produces a language of signifiers that dominate speech. When the other is marked as "enemy," called "animal," or treated as an "abject," these coded words of hatred reproduce a form of discourse that power takes. The signifiers "enemy" and "animal" are used in times of war and conflict as a weapon. The discourse of hatred always constitutes an enemy; there is no hatred without an enemy whose abjectedness (its exclusion), by contempt, degradation, and pity, ties between fear and desire, that ambivalent absent language which must be denied in order for the enemy to remain an enemy. In what follows, I will briefly present a short theoretical discussion, sort of a dictionary formulation, for these three concepts, enemy, animal, and the abject, to highlight the psycholinguistic layers of hatred and to open the hermeneutic field of hatred to the hidden markers and forces of contradiction and repression operating within relations and acts of hatred.

The Enemy and Enmity

The enemy is the lost friend. That statement, however, requires careful elaboration. The code word "enemy" is a condensed name, a signification which produces an ensemble of effects mostly known as processes of othering, exclusion, abjection, animalization, distancing, opposition, rejection, aggression, and so forth. I argue, however, that this one-track featuring is only part of the picture and not the whole of it. The lost friend is also at the same time the desired friend. And it is desire, lost and symptomized, that forms the ideology of hatred as a defensive discourse.

The enemy in classical political theory is the *inimicus*—that person who is not a friend, the antithesis of a friend—who marks the most basic distinction between life and death.[12] Schmitt defines the political itself on the basis of this polarity between friend and enemy; it is a fundamental category of the sovereign state.[13] He uses the distinction between enemy and friend to underscore the difference between the political (signified by the opposition enemy/friend) and other social domains such as the moral (good/bad), the economic (profitable/unprofitable), or the aesthetic (beautiful/ugly).[14] In contrast to this fundamental, natural opposition, what the discursive approach focuses on is the transgressive production of language.[15] To claim what one *is*, is "neither true nor false" and only indicates a system of naming.[16] I am not saying that a distinction between enemy and friend is emotionally and conceptually useless, or empirically false. I am saying that the meanings of distinction and opposition demarcate two different modes of social logic. Psychoanalytically the logic of opposition (such as that between enemy and friend) is a mirage of language, mirroring the need of people (and states) for unity, wholeness and homogeneity. But as the public discourse of enmity spreads, each individual, including citizens, can become a potential enemy, a suspect and target of surveillance and punishment. At any time, and without any warning, any immigrant worker, stateless person, or "suspicious type," citizen or not, can be legally (or illegally) persecuted under state laws and their exceptions. The word "enemy" operates like magic; once a person (or group) is labeled "the enemy," he or she is robbed instantaneously of his or her body and identity, becoming an object of state control. The word "enemy" operates as a regulatory signifier that dominates the national discourse, serving as a weapon against an entire community, which becomes an identity group because of its very name.[17] To denote the enemy, one only has to point: "he is the enemy." Enmity and hatred have transitive relations: one who is addressed as "enemy" is also one who is hated, and the hated is already the enemy. Moreover, addressing a group as "enemy" defines boundaries of exclusion. But this is where paradox enters the spaces of discourse and politics, as to be excluded one must a priori be included. Enmity (national, ethnic, and religious), like hatred or desire and death, already represents a swirl of affiliations even as it excludes the other, blurring the distinction between what must be repressed and expressed, preserved and destroyed. The question is therefore not whether (democratic) politics can exist without an enemy or with no exclusions, but rather how the definition of the enemy forms the lines of escape for possible yet impossible friendship.

The logic of difference (but not opposition) between exclusion and inclusion is the same logic that rules the difference between enemy and friend, a difference that, as Derrida has pointed out, is always already within the order of the Same (the order of language). It is a logic that says that without proximity and similarity there is no difference; it is the logic of Freudian "science," which shows that there is no love without hate and vice versa. Derrida (using the deconstructive method) similarly argues that one becomes an enemy because one is already a friend. I further elaborate on this contradictory linguistic paradox in Chapter 5. Here I note that those who are hated are always those who doubly must be within, once as the friend and once the enemy.

Recently the *New York Times* published an article on the book *Germany Does Away with Itself*, which was written by Thilo Sarrazin, a banker and former Berlin finance minister who accuses Muslim immigrants of "dumbing down" Germany's progressive society. While most "political leaders quickly condemned Sarrazin as racist," the book itself, the article goes on to say, "is already in its fourth printing with sales expected to exceed 150,000 copies."[18] The *New York Times* article underscores the fact that in spite of the quick condemnation of the book and its author by officials, there is at the same time wide agreement among most Germans that the book is picking up on a serious and "real" problem. This split language of political correctness, recognizing both hatred and shame simultaneously, is similar to the split of enemy/friend, and signifies what we tend so often to misrecognize in politics: the transgressive language of ideology. Hence, signifying the other as enemy is not only a declaration of war. It deeply affects the collective psyche through the internalization of loss, loss of friendship as a dominant politics.

The Animal and Animalization

Like use of the term "enemy," 'animal' (pointed toward a person) is a linguistic code of hatred. Usually a particular animal species is specified. Yet not just any animal will do; the enemy is never animalized as an eagle, a lion, an ox, or the leviathan—the graceful, wise, and powerful animals—but rather as a cockroach, snake, pig, behemoth, or rat. The Tutsi were called "cockroaches" by the Hutu, the Palestinians are often called "snakes" by Jewish-Israelis, and the Jews were called "pigs" or "rats" by the Nazis. These animals represent the dirty, repulsive, nonhuman nature of man. When they are applied to humans, such appellations constitute a license to attack, exclude, or destroy the other. Why do animals repulsive to man serve as a popular means of warfare, insult, and injury? How does animalizing the enemy work as an ideology of hatred?

In *The Open: Man and Animal*, Agamben questions anthropocentric Western thinking, which he terms "the politics of the anthropological machine"—the politics of animalizing the human and humanizing the animal (two variants of the same machine). Man, notes Agamben, is the only being (animal) that must recognize itself as human to be human, and must also recognize itself in a nonhuman to be human. In the Western sciences and philosophy, claims Agamben, man was recognized as human only by "animalizing the human, by isolating the nonhuman within the human."[19] There is a mobile border between the animal and human within man and "without this intimate caesura," he writes, "the very decision of what is human, and what is not, would probably not be possible."[20] "But if this is true," he continues, "if the caesura between human and the animal passes first of all within man, then it is the very question of man—and of 'humanism'—that must be posed in a new way."[21]

In Agamben's view, the imbalance of this separation is what ultimately made the Holocaust possible, and it is showing itself again today in prison camps, refugee camps, genocide, and ethnic cleansing. The danger lies in the way humanity manages its own animality—the way the anthropological machine produces the sense of humanity by suspending and closing *the animal* within—and in having to decide periodically between man and animal. These processes depict the incongruity of the caesura or its collapse; humanity "closes itself to its own openness . . . , forgets its *humanitas*, and makes being its specific disinhibitor."[22] Modernism released the nonhuman within man; Jews, Rwandans, and Palestinians became animals in human form (rats, pigs, cockroaches, and so on) within a spreading discourse of enmity that is "dragging the possibility of the distinction [between man and animal] to its ruin."[23] According to Agamben, the clash between man's animality and humanity is perhaps the most critical conflict facing Western politics today.[24] More than ever before, the relationship between man and animal must be questioned. We must ask ourselves "in what way—within man—has man been separated from non-man, and the animal from the human." On the answer(s) to this question the very fate of the human depends, he claims. Even if we do not prioritize our struggles, the collapse of the caesura between the human and the nonhuman has to become our worry.

Defining humanity against the nonhuman within man is what constitutes the enemy as nonhuman and therefore subject to a legitimized brutality. In Rwanda, Serbia, Darfur, Congo, Palestine, and so on, the legitimacy to hate has been based on the very treatment of the Other as being less than human. As such, the enemy, having assumed the image of a repulsive animal, can be confined within walls and fences, if not destroyed. This form of schizoid hatred, splitting between the human (us) and the nonhuman (them), disastrously collapses the human and the nonhuman. Or, to paraphrase Agamben, the animalization of the other, or positing one's own group as human and the other as animal, gives humanism its inhuman face. When we create life without memory (the repressed and lost memory of the friend), signifying the other as "animal" comes right back at us like a boomerang: quickly one becomes the victim of one's own victimizing introjections; one becomes an animal. Hatred, signified by enmity and by animalizing the enemy, calls for philosophical and theoretical reflection (that is, criticism) of man fearing its humanness, its desire for love and dependency, or the politics of the psyche.

The Abject

Abjection is perhaps the most rudimentary form of hatred and its unconscious phantom; it is clearly the concept that comes closest to depicting prohibited desire. Julia Kristeva is the scholar most closely associated with the noun "abjection" and the adjective "abject." In *The Power of Horror*, she connects the power of abjection (the horror of desire) to literature, motherhood, and fascism.[25] Kristeva sees abjection as that uncanny force which shapes the social (religious, political, or sexual) order, fractures and wounds systems of speech and relations, and threatens identities, when pushed under extreme conditions from the dark depths of the unconscious to the surface of language and politics. The strict boundaries between self and other within man are what separate order from the collapse of order, the internal from the external. The abject, like the animal, signifies the horror of the other, which masks itself within the social in various defensive and disguised ways of control. The abject "cuts the flesh" of the social and the national; it must be locked inside the in-group, repressed and controlled in order to maintain unity, stability, the status quo, and the sensible. The concept of the abject signifies that which cannot be signified, the full emptiness of intelligibility, the horror of the unknown yet felt, the pain that has no name or borders; it means death in life, the enchantment of death.

All societies have their Other demonic abject, but not every society fights its demons to death. Not every regime is haunted by an ideology of death. The difference lies in the distinction between various systems of libidinal economies: the need to rule that which cannot be understood and the perverse pleasure accruing from the attachment to the abhorred. In this sense abjection enacts attraction and repulsion in tandem.[26] For example, one cannot understand fascism, writes Kristeva, without making the horror and enchantment of destruction, the intimacy with death inherent in fascist ideologies, intelligible. In 1933, under extreme circumstances, fascism's abjection (ideology of death) set loose the Nazi killing machine. Agamben and Kristeva reverberate here. Can we not say that every oppressive rule, under extreme conditions, endangers its own society with the ecstasy of catastrophe, sometimes moments too late to keep from tumbling into the abyss? Watching features and documentaries on the Rwanda genocide, one cannot ignore the ecstasy of killing. In a very different way, but still disturbing and alarming, are the dancing Jewish soldiers in Hebron, shown on YouTube, not a perverse picture of the ecstasy of control? Are they dancing before or after killing? Certainly, the dance says to the Palestinian population (and the rest of the world): "We can do whatever we want here." Obviously, not everyone would agree with this interpretation. For many the dance was "cute," a message of love and humanism, showing the "human face" of the soldiers. There was widespread approval of their actions within Israel. However, it is disturbing that the dancing soldiers were discussed in isolation from the context of the Occupation, without mention of place, Hebron, and their dance was seen simply as a naïve performance. It further shows how libidinal pleasure, produced by the war machine, can be overlooked, or looked "cute." This celebration of power, the collapsed boundaries between abjection and humanism, the unconscious politics of desire, is what I call the ideology of hatred embodied by the dancing soldiers. Just try to imagine the horror and repulsion of the Palestinians watching from their windows. I would not deny that such an invasive act, the dancing soldiers in Hebron, is not at the same time also seductive. This is, however, precisely how abjection enunciates its repulsive attraction.

The enemy, animal, and abject press together a concept of hatred that resists a language of desire for the other, returning as ecstasy and death. While most scholars of ethnic and national conflicts are concerned with what is obvious in hatred—separation, distance, destruction—my own concern is with the unknown and the impossible, paradoxes of exclusion and inclusion, disgust and delight, eroticism and death, expressions of transgressing the edge, and hatred as disguise to what must be collectively silenced and denied, the need for what must be excluded from the group (social, national, or political) consciousness.

After many sociological, anthropological, psychological, and linguistic attempts to explain and understand power relations, the fear of the other still remains a puzzle. Why, Sara Ahmed asks, does the "other" who is brought into the sphere of our existence become a threat?[27] Is it because of our need of the other and yet, at the same time, our fear and dread of the desire of the other? Does the ideology of hatred signify the unconscious of discourse and politics? The concept of the political unconscious (which I discuss in Chapter 2)—the desirous libidinal politics of the enemy-friend split— suggests that politics and the unconscious are two different regimes, but not two different territories. According to Wohl, every text has an unconscious—an internal other that rewrites the text from within.[28] By contrast Deleuze claims that "politics is in the unconscious itself," relating directly to an entire social field.[29] While these two different approaches to the unconscious might seem contradictory, Wohl's oedipal analysis of ideology and Deleuze's anti-oedipal analysis, if mitigated through a view of events as both phantasmal and concrete, suggest that social reality is shaped by the unconscious of the text and the text of the unconscious in tandem. One could say that the unconscious operates in itself and out of itself, within the psyche and in the world, *in* and *as* discourse.

The Political Unconscious

In this chapter I focus on developing the concept of the political unconscious.[1] My main purpose is methodological: to establish the relations between discourse and the unconscious or, more precisely, to outline the
unconscious elements of discourse and draw attention to the power of unconscious desires, which are already social and normative yet propagate a
discourse of libidinal national and ethnic conflict. The readers will obviously realize the circular nature of this argument or ask themselves: What
could be the unconscious of discourse? Does discourse have an unconscious? After all, is it not the power of discourse that forms the subject and
subjectivity? To this parable of politics and life I now turn.

A few scholars have offered a theoretical psychoanalytic interpretation
of the unconscious power of discourse, and this chapter is certainly framed
into the dialogue of their work.[2] Lacan's influence is of course undeniable.
Yet hatred is neither an entire text nor an obvious discourse, neither unseen
nor obviously seen. What is missing from or foreclosed in national dis-

course that forms the circularity of hate discourse and the psyche? How do hate speech and hating articulate not only the power of the unconscious but also the power of the discourse of the unconscious? I do not mean to suggest simply that hate discourses repress narratives of forbidden love, but that national conflicts are a symptom of desire which is left unexpressed or disconnected to its phantasmatic source; that group and individual desire is unrecognized and refused in response to national discourse and its social control, and consequently desire is manifested as collective hatred.

The perspective of desire suggests that the question we should ask regarding intractable conflicts is: What attachments does national discourse deny and disavow? If, as Freud argued, "the data of consciousness are exceedingly defective" and mental acts often can be explained only on the basis of other acts, of which consciousness yields no evidence,[3] and if we agree, as Victoria Wohl suggests, that the political always has a demanding unconscious,[4] then the topography of the political unconscious and its desires requires our full attention. In particular, we need to understand those desires that take shape as fantasies of prohibited identifications, fantasies on the order of "what if." *If* I become like the other, or dependent on the other, or *if* I allow myself to love the other, what might happen? Even when desires are repressed and denied, Freud suggests that they still determine and constitute the nature and course of enmity and friendship in the field of the political.[5]

To study the unconscious of hatred or rather the ideology of hatred (recontextualized as a veiled discourse of desire) is not to say that hatred is unconscious or invisible. On the contrary, hatred is a forceful embodied experience, and even when not always admitted and spoken, it is felt, projected, and acted upon. At the same time, the ideology of hatred is constituted through unconscious forces that repeat and reproduce that which is absent from the discourse of hatred yet not erased from it. Blaming, animalizing, and at times killing the other is a symptom similar to what Freud calls "organ speech," standing in for an impossible object-cathexis. Does not the fact that some national conflicts and racial or ethnic hatreds become obsessive struggles or the fact that "simple" (and indeed solvable) territorial disputes become passionate wars impossible to untangle and defuse indicate that, in such cases, hate relations signal that something more is going on? Disagreement and difference, even when deep and strong, are not the entire story of intractable conflicts; unconscious desires must be considered. Operating as forbidden "thoughts" and complicating recognition and communication, hatred, in addition to being a system of discursive control, carries *a message*. And if we wish to understand hate relations, this message has to be decoded and articulated, not only by what hatred says but also by what hatred wants. It is difficult to avoid slipping back and forth between hate discourse and hate relations. This slippage is, however, endemic to libidinal systems that, like desire, form the subjectivity of the political.[6]

My use of the term "political unconscious" is based on Freud's general conception of the unconscious as the region of psychic prohibitions (censorships, in his language) that operates in ways that divert, displace, repeat, reproduce, split, repress, or act out forbidden desires.[7] This definition is, of course, already a misreading of Freud's concept, or a translation of sorts. Invoking the term "prohibition" rather than "censorship" to describe the operations of the unconscious already presupposes that the unconscious is first and foremost a "discursive unconscious" (rather than a mechanical moral gatekeeper), which consents to the laws of culture and society. Prohibitions are not only normative proscriptions of behavior ("do" and "do not" imperatives), but a form of interpellating calls; a secretive pact with the sovereign, a quiet "enlistment" of the subject, a call for loyalty to the sovereign, to refuse the love of the other before loving. In a memorable yet opaque utterance, Freud claims, "The mental, like the physical, is not necessarily in reality just what it appears to us to be." This Kantian conclusion (and indeed Freud cites Kant) is, however, not that simple. If we emphasize the physical in the sentence (rather than the mental), considering it also to metaphorically represent material reality (and not only the physical body), we could, by inference, reread this sentence, suggesting that (social and political) reality presents itself through processes that are already covered and unseen, already repressed or denied, that what we must see is not what we see, and that what should not have happened did happen and therefore must be denied by law. Perhaps Freud would have said that as long as we believe that only visible, observable, and measurable faculties count as reality, understanding (mental, physical, and social) reality will always remain illusory and lead to misrecognition. In some ways we can say that Freud "discovered" the political unconscious.[8]

Indeed, Freud's social psychology, particularly in *Group Psychology, Civilization and Its Discontents, Totem and Taboo*, and *Beyond the Pleasure Principle*, reflects his effort to delineate an archeology of a "group unconscious." A group's unconscious produces illusions, fantasies, and denials, but it also protects the normative order and the social conventions, reassuring (ensuring), in Foucault's terms, the power of the law and social discipline. One, although perhaps not the most popular, way to read Freud's social psychology is that the unconscious comes into being as the guardian of the norm: in the absence of a fence, there can be no dreams of crossing it, and without the power of normativity, desire has no signifiers. If the Law (the master signifier) dictates forbidden relations, does it not also provoke fantasies of the impossible? Although this is in reverse logic to Freud's elaboration of the incest taboo,[9] Freud's articulation of the id, the ego, and the superego as an interconnected system of prohibitions and his emphasis on the failure of the Law to impose constraints on sexual desire raise political questions, such as: What does the other want from me, and what do I want of the other? What do I want of my friend and enemy? These questions that are addressed toward the other ask not about the "object" of desire (land, for example) and its economy, but about those signifying processes that transform the "object" into a forbidden relation, into a sign of and a signifying post to the desire of the other. Freud's understanding of the social teaches that the law (the familial law), that which bounds desire to the norm, signifies its "secret" failure and that the power of the law marks its impossibility in the order of the necessary.

In *Totem and Taboo* as well as in *Group Psychology and the Analysis of the Ego*, Freud reconstructs the first "historical" moment of group repression and forgetting. The genesis of the unconscious begins with violence—the murder of the father (the beloved father and the enemy at once) by the sons—and the repression of the desire for the father. On the one hand, violence allowed the sons to declare the dead father the sovereign and ensure the preservation of his memory and name through identification. With the sons' avowal, the first social law was born—the Law of the father. But the law was not constituted only, as some interpreters have claimed, in order to prevent future violence or to guarantee the loyalty of the sons to each other. The first law was established on the ruins of desire and on its prohibiting punitive guilt.[10] And so the guilt ensured not only the power of the father but also the prohibition of the desire of the enemy. Repression, according to Freud, is the key, although not the only, organizer of the unconscious, and it certainly does not comprise the whole unconscious.[11] Repression according to Freud is a dynamic force, a continuing *struggle* with desire and prohibition without which social life would become unfathomable.[12] History, politics, and culture thus start at the moment in which the unconscious is formed. Freud makes it clear that the unconscious—the topography of repression—is the formative structure of a community, its possibility and horizon. Built on aggression and guilt, desire and punishment, the unconscious is the locus of both the subject's phantasmatic desire and the internalized prohibiting norm. Moreover, the struggle between desire and prohibition means that the condition of possibility for individual repression is the preexistence of the group.

Freud's eclipsed topology of desire and prohibition is the working basis of the political unconscious. It was Lacan, however, who understood Freud's unarticulated and un-spelled-out political unconscious and brought it into focus (yet not into naming). Lacan's reading of Freud indicates that once the structure of the unconscious is perceived as the structure of language, desire has an effect but no reality beyond the signifier. Desire must be conceived as the desire of the Other bounded and controlled by the Law of the father (or the tyrant, the sovereign, the leader), the law that frames the workings of the unconscious. For Freud, the unconscious belongs to the symbolic order already bound to the demands of the language of prohibitions.[13] Lacan, however, in contrast to Freud, establishes a fundamental gap in the heart of the unconscious; the Real—desire untouched by language and symbolization—and the symbolic—desire signified by the laws of discourse. In this very gap, Lacan inscribed the politics of the self in the field of the other. Even if we do not necessarily accept the notion of the Real (the phantomized but not the fantasized desire), we can still say that the demands of desire, but particularly its signifying effects in discourse, are after all what politics is all about (or what groups covertly fight about).

The desire *of* the other (which is also *to* and *for* the other) articulates the unconscious of hatred and the place of the other's desire (as well as desire to and for the other) in the politics of national conflicts. In psychoanalysis, the desire to be loved by the other but also to own the pleasure of the other is a fundamental human need of existence. In political relations, the will to "have" and "own" the desire of the other implies a control over the "enjoyment" of the other, a power over the desire of the other. This is perhaps the most fundamental fantasy of power in politics—to control the pleasure of the other, to forcibly elicit compliance and servitude in the name of "democratic love."[14] This ontological fantasy has its price, namely, our own inevitable dependencies on the other whom we so wish to control. This double bind of desire (controlling and being controlled) means that we are never really fully in control. Hence, I argue, the desire of the other becomes the "master signifier" of conflict; on the one hand to control what the other "wants," on the other hand "wanting" to be loved by the other as a "proof' " (that we owe to ourselves as subjects of humanism) of our justness and goodness.[15] At the same time, the idea of dependency on the rival other and seeking the love of the enemy is (in the economy of power) an unthinkable thought, a horrifying thought, the consciousness of the "unthought" that was already thought and denied, an absence that threatens to undo the (national) subject, leaving its transformed marks on reality only through obsessive acts and hate discourses. The denial of attachment creates symptomatic relations which revolve around repeated prejudices, misrecognitions, and failures of communicative language. Desire becomes the "blind spot" of conflict around which injurious acts are constituted and carried out. This suggests that a whole "community of unconsciousness"[16] is built not only, as Bourdieu has suggested, upon repressed memories but also on shared denials and discursive projections of disavowal; that hatred is constituted not only around demands for land, autonomy, or freedom but also as a necessary part of national ideology, which conceals unconscious signifiers of dependency and desire, circulating a power politics of disavowal.

Circulating a power politics of disavowal has been discussed in different yet connected ways by Foucault, Žižek, and Butler, who explore, each in their own theoretical language and aims, the claim that unthought desire—that discursive suture, which particularly in relations of conflict becomes invisible, inconceivable, and unthinkable—constitutes an ideology of hatred as a symptom of its reality. Even though Foucault, Žižek, and Butler do not engage the term "the political unconscious," their philosophical and political writings provide insightful and provocative ideas that are theoretically important and relevant to understanding the concept of the political unconscious. In the rest of the chapter I turn to a close reading of their texts.

Foucault and the Cultural Unconscious (or "Whatever Name We Give It")

It is known that Foucault was opposed to the concept of the unconscious, particularly in its oedipal formulation. Foucault's readers generally agree that Foucault resisted a separate notion of the psyche and "psychic power,"[17] of internality and externality, and in fact was never seduced by psychoanalysis.[18] But, as I will show, Foucault was much more ambivalent toward psychoanalysis and the unconscious than he was willing to admit. On the one hand, he denounced the unconscious as a product of the psychoanalytic discourse of a psychic inner life. On the other hand, he attributed to the unconscious a different status within the psychological sciences, namely, as a structure of systems that, while possessing a conceptual normalizing power, also has the potential to disturb the meaning of internality (and internal life) and the relations between history and subjectivity. Thus, in spite of Foucault's resistance to psychoanalysis as a science of finitude, he assigned to Freud (and to psychoanalysis) a special place within the "normalizing sciences."[19] He believed that, in contrast to the other anthropological sciences of man, Freud took a different methodological path toward interrogating man and reflecting on truth. His ambivalence itself suggests a critical road map directing us to reread the concept of the unconscious *in* discourse and *as* discourse.

In a discussion on psychiatry, Foucault said: "When people have their own space and consequently find it easier to escape or ignore the political apparatus, or to hide from it, how will they be caught? They'll be caught on the couch, in psychotherapy, etc."[20] This cynical quotation demonstrates Foucault's perception of psychotherapy as a normalizing apparatus together with the rest of the human sciences (anthropology, sociology, economics, history, psychology, etc.), which "invented," as he claimed, man in the nineteenth century: "We are so blinded by the recent manifestation of man that we can no longer remember a time—and it is not so long ago—when the world, its order, and human beings existed, but man did not."[21] These sciences, which he often called the anthropological sciences, have created a referential (representational) distance between the *idea* and the *sign*, which stopped being transparent to each other, instigating a taken-for-granted dichotomy between internal and external knowledge, thinking and speaking, seeing and saying, the visible and the invisible. In particular he was opposed to the scientific endeavor of searching for man's true nature in order to advance a better man, purer and free.

Foucault criticized the neutralization and naturalization of man, that is, the stripping of the individual from the codes governing language and cultural institutions. Moreover, if taken at face value, psychoanalysis, as part of the human sciences, is a landscape that can never be reached by the reflection of the subject or his or her consciousness.[22] In a critical tone, Foucault wrote: "The whole of modern thought is imbued with the necessity of thinking the unthought—of reflecting the contents of the In-itself in the form of the For-itself, of ending men's alienation by reconciling him with his own essence."[23] Modern Man, he further argued, cannot think of himself without an element of darkness, of inert destiny that is always in relation to the Other. Thus, the unconscious was for Foucault a marked region of haunted thoughts (his way to describe the inner psyche), which has through its conceptualization and treatment confined man to power relations of psychiatric control and alienation.

This criticism comes with the analysis of the modern *cogito* that "does not reduce the whole being of things to thought without ramifying the being of thought right down to the inert network of what does not think." Since the nineteenth century, the unthought has accompanied man mutely and wholly as a mode of being, "being in that dimension where thought addresses the unthought and articulates itself upon it."[24] This articulation echoes Foucault's genealogical analysis of modern reason and particularly the place of madness in it, defined as that which does not think. Indeed, in *Madness and Civilization*, Foucault places psychoanalysis (putting it on trial, as Derrida claims) within the psychiatric and medical tradition of cure in the nineteenth century.[25] He saw psychoanalysis as an anthropological exploration in search of a better, objective, and universal man. He accused Freud of enhancing a language of prohibition that created a split within the utterance of madness between what it says and what it means, "a silent surplus that quietly enunciates what it says." The concept of madness—a linguistic code that has no meaning; that does not say anything but itself—

became a case of a structurally esoteric language that articulates "something else beneath what it says," something that is a meaningless logos and an excluded language.[26] The search for the unconscious and unconscious desire is, like the deployment of sexuality, part of the very effective disciplinary technology of the modern discourse of man.

But this angry response is only part of the picture. Foucault was not always so decisive in his criticism of Freud and psychoanalysis. In the last chapter of *The Order of Things*, Foucault presents a softer and more appreciative perspective. Derrida advanced the argument that Foucault's relation to Freud and the Freudian moment in history was confused, ambivalent, and contradictory: "Sometimes he wants to credit Freud, sometimes discredit him, unless he is actually doing both indiscernibly and at the same time."[27] Obviously, Foucault could not have totally closed himself or been indifferent to the psychoanalytic project, the most influential theory of subjectivity since the nineteenth century. But Derrida was much more decisive: "Would Foucault's project have been possible without psychoanalysis?" he asks.[28]

On the one hand, Foucault accuses psychoanalysis of situating itself in the dimension of the unconscious, of developing a system of hidden knowledge that must speak itself by "making the discourse of the unconscious speak through consciousness"; he disputes the definition of desire as the unthought at the heart of thought, which means that all significations have an origin and the return of this origin is promised in analysis.[29] He also contends that psychoanalysis sustains the patient's alienation in the hierarchical doctor-patient power relations. On the other hand, Foucault credits psychoanalysis (and ethnology) with a privileged position within the human sciences, stemming from the fact that psychoanalysis does not pretend to present a general theory of man—and can, in fact, almost do without the concept of man. He claims that it provides knowledge of man only within the limits of praxis, that it observes itself, calling into question its own ambitions and functions, and, most of all, that the psychoanalyst (and psychoanalysis as a system) listens to the language of the other, the language of madness.

Truly, psychoanalysis, as part of the human sciences, reproduces the Western representations of madness and irrationality, but in contrast to the human sciences, which "advance toward the unconscious only with their back to it," psychoanalysis goes toward the unconscious by listening to the patient's language, not in order to liberate man or excavate what lies behind his or her thoughts, but to let the patient know the rules that govern his or her needs and desire. Psychoanalysis (at its "best") does not question man, but circles the topography of desire, law (language), and death as the designating regions and the conditions of possibility of knowledge about man.[30] In that sense, although the unconscious points to the existence of mute texts, "of a blank space in a visible text," in contrast to the human sciences, psychoanalysis looks at the unconscious in a different way, not by "waiting for it to unveil itself as fast as consciousness is analyzed," but by recognizing its inaccessibility and listening to "the disruptive image of a signifier that is *absolutely not* [italics in the original] like the others."[31] At some point, Foucault even suggests seeing psychoanalysis as a counter-science.

One can clearly see why Derrida has pointed to the contradictions in Foucault's love/hate relation with psychoanalysis. What I believe surfaces, however, is Foucault's distinction between two systems of psychoanalysis: psychoanalysis that belongs to the anthropological sciences of finitude that seek to better man, and psychoanalysis that attempts not to cure or improve man, but rather to understand the language of subjectivity within the historicity of the norm.

So far, I have summarized Foucault's relation to psychoanalysis as a field of knowledge that is simultaneously part of the Western *episteme* and a challenge to it. I further suggest that some of Foucault's ideas, such as the power of discourse or the disciplinary society, veil or even hide a necessary language of the unconscious, that the inter-text of these concepts recognizes the necessary power of the psyche. In light of his criticism of the human sciences and anthropological psychology, it is plausible that Foucault tried to avoid using the concept of the unconscious in order to shield his work from psychological interpretations. All the same, in *The Order of Things* he articulates a concept of the unconscious without using the word in any substantial way. Toward the end, in a brief outline rather than a fully developed idea, he advances the concept of the "cultural unconscious," suggesting (but never quite saying) that cultures must have an unconscious. From this outline at the end of *The Order of Things* but also from other short comments in his interviews and lectures,[32] one might conclude that Foucault was using the "cultural unconscious" in reference to an invisible structure of prohibitions on thought, that like Freud he was talking about a structure that subjects man to invisible yet possible knowledge. He saw both psychoanalysis and ethnology as sciences of the unconscious in that they signify the Law of society: the working systems of a specific culture and the invisible rules and norms that govern expression. Clearly such a subversive concept of the unconscious—as a signifying system that cannot be produced by the activity of consciousness—was part of Foucault's concept of discourse and language.[33] Echoing Freud, he says: "Humanity does not start out from freedom but from limitation and the line not to be crossed." We know, he continues, the rules that constitute forbidden acts. "But we still do not know much about the organization of the prohibitions in language."[34] So what are these prohibitions in language (the thought of the unthought) if not the Freudian definition of the unconscious?

It is, I believe, the above statement that is most revealing and the closest Foucault came to articulating the place of the unconscious in discourse. In this utterance he opened a small crack to the unconscious at the level of language that is not allowed to show itself in thought, yet is a form of knowledge—not because that knowledge is repressed or buried, but because the unconscious is a "cover operation" in the service of discourse; a linguistic regime that, like all power regimes (military, governmental, or psychiatric), operates by means of its own barriers and measures of control.[35] On these grounds, it would be fair to say that Foucault, like Freud and Lacan, advanced a concept of the unconscious as a "policing" system that operates by other means; a region of (unconscious, perhaps rebellious) "dangerous thoughts" that must be excluded and concealed from consciousness and from our relation to truth in the field of the other. What I mean to say here is that the unconscious is not only topography of desire but also the means by which desire shows in language.[36] At the same time, when desire is expressed in language it always appears, as Freud insisted, in forms other than itself and by means that play on its subversive meanings by transforming the signs and signifiers of desire into enigmatic objects or into "safe" subjects. The signifier of "unsafe" love, for example, would be a "joyful" or, in the eyes of the subject, a justified hatred.

What do Foucault's few positive remarks on the unconscious teach us? What can we conclude from his preference for speaking about invisible signifiers, interior to consciousness, or cover-up operations as a substitute rhetorical strategy? I suggest that this move accommodates a wider and more complex notion of discipline and power, that along with the means submerged within the discourse of war and hatred, such as incarceration, confinement, or expulsion, there operates an invisible system within discourse, an oppositional "secret language" organized to reconstitute and (safely) reassure the order of things. But does this view open a new possibility of understanding the ideology of hatred? To answer these questions, I shall continue to explore Žižek's concept of ideology and Butler's theory of subjection and subjectivity in order to assemble a clearer understanding of hate politics as an apparatus of power involved in a "cover operation."

Žižek's Ideological Desire

Žižek is perhaps the most unequivocal proponent of the unconscious apparatus, of its power and theoretical usefulness for understanding contemporary politics, conflicts, and animosity. To understand Žižek's political and cultural position, we must pay close attention to how he revives Marx's concept of ideology through Lacanian language and Lacan's concepts of the symbolic and the pre-symbolic Real—the "primordially repressed" (the *objet petit a*), which does not change under the pressures of culture.[37] Žižek turns the un-symbolized Real into an active political force, speaking of the way in which the Real becomes a symptom, an ideological desire. For Žižek, the symbolization and interpretation of the Real—the "hard kernel of desire" that resists symbolization—grips the ideological moment, that moment in which desire becomes signified and the Real becomes a spectral apparition. More simply stated, symbolization is a moment of failure to see the return of the repressed, the leaks of the Real into reality, the Real of antagonism between desire and the norm. To delineate the idea of the political unconscious using Žižek's notion of ideology, it is necessary to magnify his ambivalence, or rather his theoretical (not to say rhetorical) maneuvers to "save" the Real, mostly known to readers of Lacan as an unchangeable (and so beyond space and time) desire for the phallus, by endowing the Real with a new political life.[38] What does that mean?

In general, we can say that for Žižek, ideology is *the mechanism that regulates the social visibility and non-visibility of desire.*[39] More specifically, and against the classical Marxian notion of false consciousness as ideology, Žižek argues that ideology has nothing to do with illusion or distorted representation. A political attitude or belief can be completely true and still ideological, he says. Ideology is not defined in relation to the truthfulness or falseness of an idea, but rather in relation to its effect, that is, to the concealed ways in which dominant ideas are legitimized. For example, we could say, as the Israeli government claimed, that the Israeli attack on Gaza was aimed at stopping Hamas from firing missiles at southern Israeli settlements. That claim was true. At the same time, the attack was also a spectral manifestation of desire to control public opinion within Israel and to legitimize the power of the state. These concealed motives are not false, but ideological. The fact that the Israeli public was kept in the dark, was denied seeing photographic images of civilian casualties from Gaza in the name of security (the ultimate signifier of ideology), immediately revealed the covert motives of the government regardless of the denials, showing how ideology pops up precisely when we attempt to hide it.[40]

At the same time, Žižek strongly urges us not to be too hasty to accept the post-structural assumption that reality is always already indistinguishable from ideology. We need to keep the tension of the critique of ideology alive, he warns. For precisely that reason, he pursues the idea of the "specter" (the return of the Real into reality). The spectral—or ideological desire—appears in the a priori gap between the Real and reality and fills the void created by that which escapes realty. But what the specter conceals is not reality but the "primordially repressed," he writes, "the irrepresentable X on whose 'repression' reality itself is founded."[41] It is, however, the fact of repression (its very necessity) that signifies the operation and the power of the norm. How might we then characterize the relations between ideology and the unconscious?

The relations between ideology and the unconscious are formed at the moment in which ideology is denounced, at the moment of its denial, when ideology becomes not a believed experience but the truth itself (when claims for security are uncritically taken for granted).[42] Such a denunciation, says Žižek, "is not 'reality' but the 'repressed' Real of antagonism."[43] Around the un-symbolized (often the traumatic), the attempt to cope with the Real of antagonism is "acted out" and becomes real (natural). The idea that the unconscious is not simply a reservoir of latent (unseen) thought but a territory of the repressed that returns as a symptom is shared by both Freud and Žižek. But Žižek goes beyond Freud's "return of the repressed," arguing that surplus desire (re)turns into a phantasmal reality (or ideology) which enunciates "true" reality.[44] Can we rethink the ideology of hatred in terms of Žižek's notion of repressed desire?

Returning to hatred, we could say that the ideology of hatred supposedly covers up something that is more horrifying than hatred itself (fantasies of attachment and dependency on the enemy can be an example). The ideology of hatred is a social symptom and the "logic" of the unknown, the logic of fear and the desire of the other that discourse must conceal and hide. Moreover, the concealment of attachment and dependency by the ideology of hatred is itself the symptom of ideological desire, that which is forbidden and must be denied by different legitimized means. Using his analysis of class struggle (capitalism's repression of class struggle and revolutionary desire) as an example, Žižek stresses that the purpose of critique is to expose the structure of ideological fantasy. It is worth noting that for Žižek the ideological fantasy is a symptom of "doing," not of "knowing." It is not what people know that counts, but how they act, he points out. For example, people know that money is only a sign; they can laugh about money, strike a cynical aloofness from it, but still act *as if* money were the embodiment of wealth and truth. Laughter is one way "to blind ourselves to the structuring power of ideological fantasy."[45] Ideological fantasy (the *as if*) gives the symptom its symbolic place in reality and frames the return of the repressed. That is why, according to Žižek, we can say that the truth (the repressed or the displaced) arises from misrecognition or from error, and that error is always part of truth itself.

But the effectiveness of the symptom is maintained only insofar as its logic is unknown to the subject. Therefore, the symptom is constructed retroactively from the future, from the system of meanings to the thing "itself." Put differently, the repressed is returning from the future, he says. This also means that the repressed, coming back from the future, is already indistinguishable not only from what the symptom says but also from what the symptom wants. Enfolded in this temporal formulation is the idea not only that the symptom is already a signifier, that is, a symbolic formation,[46] but also that the symptom "wants" at any price to protect the norm and its subjects of interpellation. If we adopt, as I do, Žižek's concept of the symptom, or the idea that the ideology of hatred is the performance, or acting out, of the fantasy of love through hatred, we can say that national conflict and hate speech conceived as a symptom represent through nationalism's overt narcissism the denied desire of the other. The persistence of war (or prejudice and hatred) is a signification of a symptomatic reality or a world where desire has become the nodal point of ideology.

What this means is that the political unconscious of hatred reveals itself in a series of effects that are always distorted from threatening possible libidinal attachments and displaced by conditional fantasies of impossibility.[47] From Žižek's analysis of the *Titanic* as a cultural symptom of grandiosity and prejudice, we learn that desire always returns in the form of a fantasy of control. That fantasy is, however, precisely the paradox of hatred: the more we fantasize about destroying the other, the more we become attached to it and out of control. Hatred is an ideology that covers up the desire of the other through a fantasy of control and normalization, a psychic imaginary in the service of power. What is still left to be reconsidered is the concept of the psyche and its workings in politics. This discussion brings us to Butler and her theory of ambivalence, which takes over where Foucault and Žižek leave off, namely, her concept of subjectivity and singularity in terms of the norm and in the norm where subjection and resistance to power form and emerge in tandem.

Butler's Melancholic (Re)Turn

In the conjunction of psychoanalysis and politics, Butler challenges Freud and Foucault on matters of private speech and social action, subordination and resistance, subjectivation and agency or, differently put, on the psychic life of power, which is the title of her book. *The Psychic Life of Power* is the central focus of my discussion here. Like Foucault and Žižek, Butler does not use the concept of the political unconscious, but her work on power, discourse, and psychic life suggests a concept of a discursive unconscious which is prima facie political.

I take as my starting point Butler's famous claim that no individual (the bearer of language and intelligibility) becomes a subject without first undergoing subjectivation, that is, becoming a subject who is produced in and through language.[48] At the heart of this process lies a gap or a fissure, albeit a "fabricated" one, "between reiteration and resistance, between the subject's emergence and the conditions of power."[49] It is a gap between two temporal modalities of power "before" and "after" the presence of the subject. "Power not only acts on a subject but in a transitive sense, enacts the subject," she writes. For agency to take place, however, subjects must resist the norm, but resistance always also takes place under the terms of subordination. Hence, for Butler, the unconscious is a site of oppositions, the subject's resistance to the very power that has constituted the subject. At the same time, power is not a fixed unity but a transgressive and dynamic social force undergoing continuous articulation: "Power rearticulated is 're'-articulated in the sense of already done and 're'-articulated in the sense of done over, done again, done anew."[50] Between "already done" and "done anew" lies the temporal gap within which the subject is constituted in discourse. In *The Psychic Life of Power*, Butler sets out to rework this gap between the being who is already there and that who is yet-to-come in an effort to suture the (philosophical) dichotomy between the political and the psychic.

That suture—drawing a knotted connection between the regulatory effects of power and the constitution of the subject—is where, in my reading, discourse and psychoanalysis meet, and the political unconscious eclipses desire and prohibition. It is, however, important to note that Butler creates this suture not by synthesis or an intermediating third concept, but rather through a circular movement of reiteration and resistance, citation and subversion, one working within the terms of the other. Hence, at the heart of discourse lies a paradox of the enactment of the subject. The question we still need to ask is in what specific ways power becomes formative and vulnerable. How does discourse both enact and exceed its power?

The tie between Freud and Foucault may not be obvious, but for Butler it opens up a field, which allows her to explore and spell out the mechanisms that language and desire employ in the unconscious. Compared with Foucault and Žižek, Butler perhaps comes closest to inscribing a psychic topography of normative power, effecting reality as an "un-present" (foreclosed) operation. Butler's critique of internalization and the linear logic of an "outside" that enters a pre-given "inside" is meant to problematize the discussion on how the power of discourse and the forces of the psyche work, each in terms of the other. Butler asks: "Does the norm, having become psychic, involve not only the interiorization of the norm, but the interiorization of the psyche?"[51] Is Butler suggesting here that discourse reconstitutes not only the internality of the subject, but the psyche itself? How, she asks "are we to account for *the desire for the norm* [italics mine] and for subjection more generally in terms of *a prior desire for social existence* [italics mine], a desire exploited by regulatory power?"[52]

A desire for the norm and subjection? Do subjects have *a desire* for the norm? In many ways her challenging question contains the answer. It posits the most fundamental kernel of human motivation—existence—as the Achilles heel of desire, the desire for the norm. It is evident here through this question that Butler, like Žižek, defines the subject in relation to the fantasy of the norm (a desire to be "normal") and considers the subject's existence to be dependent on his and her subordination to that fantasy. The internalization of the norm—the subject's turning to the norm in submission to safeguard its conditions of existence—is the constitutive moment of the psyche, the moment in which the subject becomes desirous in a specific way. Needless to say, the norm never fully takes control over the person, yet every norm, and this is the definition of the norm, has its habitual power. That mode of "belonging to power," that particular form of existence, Butler calls *melancholic existence*. Melancholy is a form of psychic subjection: an apparatus for subduing panic, constraining difference, and regulating the terms of the norm. Melancholy signifies the psychic operation of the norm—in fact, the working of a political unconscious that enunciates the effective prohibition of the norm and its successful regulation of desire but also the loss of both the other and the possibility of democratic love.

Butler identifies Lacan's notion of *foreclosure*—a prohibition or denial of desire, its lost (but not erased) traces—as the main mechanism of psychic subjection. It singles out the contingency between reality and psychic operation of the norm as two inseparable, albeit different, forms of expression. Hence the norm already contains a "lost" desire of the other. Under conditions of melancholic incorporation, the mechanism of foreclosure operates in dual circles: on the one hand it rejects the loss of the object of desire, but on the other hand it authorizes normalization and submission to the norm. Melancholia simultaneously features the psychic site of both resistance and submission. Butler's political understanding of desire and the psyche, but even more so her emphasis on the effects of melancholy on reality, from unconscious grieving to resentment to outright hatred and violence,[53] changes the theoretical ground for understanding how "certain kinds" of objects are recognized and others misrecognized, how some are loved and others are sanctioned from love, or the love of them becomes unthinkable. Foreclosed love (but we could also think of attachment or dependency), says Butler, operates as a desire that was "never owned" and yet lived by multiple signs. Repudiated identifications (whether sexual, national, or class related), as a form of existence, depict the life of a lost desire. The important point to note here is that, for Butler, "love that is out of question" does not fail to leave a mark on reality; love that never happened can still take on "cultural dimensions of contemporary consequence."

Perhaps the most instructive point to be taken from Butler's concept of repudiation is her insistence on seeing the psyche not simply as an internal storage of "good" and "bad" objects, admitted from the outside to the inside through various modes of internalization, but as a matrix of foreclosed attachments, which require the preservation of the lost object of repudiation "as its own most treasured source of sustenance."[54] If the subject is produced, as Butler stresses, in discourse that is not its own production, and if the renunciation of the other occurs in order to "cover up" for the lost but not erased desire of the other, what becomes clear is that the mechanism of foreclosure not only partakes in the reproduction of the law by engaging the law,[55] but signifies the psychic unconscious power of discourse in the same way that "ideological desire" and "discursive desire" designate the symptomatic reality of the Real. Thus, the discourse of the psyche (the politics of foreclosure and return) is the foundational turn of melancholia.[56]

Is she saying that psychic life returns to regulate social life? If we follow Butler's "logic" to the end, it becomes clear that the melancholic turn, which is the moment of subjection and subjectivity, takes place within neither a preexisting internality nor a pre-constituted external reality, nor in some third space, but in social reality itself, which is confounded by the loss of the object (of love) and by its preservation. The melancholic *turn* is conditioned by its repudiation and by the melancholic conditions themselves. Discourse already includes the unknown, that which is withdrawn from consciousness. And this return of the unknown is constituted as part of the conditions of possibility. "The internal topography by which melancholia is partially explained is itself the effect of that melancholy."[57] But melancholia does not have an external point of departure, Butler warns. It becomes clear that melancholia "produces the possibility for the representation of psychic life,"[58] by signifying the unthinkable, the unknown loss. Melancholia produces rhetorical subversions and organizes "the field of the speakable." Take, for example, national hatred. Can we say that in order to simultaneously denote and deny attachment, foreclosed desire (of the other) returns to the field of relations as violent, distractive, and genocidal hatred? That the failure to resist necessary but lost attachments constitutes who we are, the kind of images of the other available to us, the institutional defenses at our disposal, and the horizon of our future community?

Foucault instructed us to pay attention to modern reason as a particular schema of knowledge, to consider the constructive power of discourse. He sensitized us to regard regimes of truth with suspicion. Nevertheless, Foucault overlooked the power of the foreclosed and disavowed. Žižek emphasized the domination of the non-symbolic, the Real, in reality. Butler, in contrast to Foucault and Žižek, evokes the psychoanalytic unconscious as a topology of foreclosed desire. She emphasizes omissions from discourse that gain authority precisely because what is denied becomes incorporated as an absence. In *The Psychic Life of Power*, Butler articulates the mechanisms and the price of disavowed knowledge that becomes a form of dominant intelligibility. Incorporating the other as an absent one who was "never loved and never lost," she articulates a process of psychic idealization in the service of discourse, or, speaking more generally, the logic, as she writes, of "never, never," which represents the symptom of discourse.

Within a given rationality, the logic of "never, never" reflects the unaddressed within the addressed. "Something is sacrificed, lost, or at least spent or given up at the moment in which the subject makes himself into an object of possible knowledge."[59] This double self-fabrication—what the subject knows and what he or she does not dare to know, what one says and what one loses at the moment of speech—is the moment of subjectivation. It is not a simple internalization of rationality, but a way of becoming a subject through the price that each of us pays for our normalization, in fact our "normality." This double subjection to the power of discourse—

conformity and loss (or sacrifice)—is what I consider the power of the political unconscious.

What do we learn from Foucault's criticism of the human sciences, from Žižek's concepts of ideology and "the symptom," and from Butler's analysis of melancholia and the subject's double subjection to power? To say that the three of them challenge (albeit in different ways) the relations between subjectivity and discourse (ideology or normativity) would be too obvious. To say that none of them takes the concept of the unconscious for granted, and all three redefine and problematize the relation between desire and knowledge, invisibility and visibility, would not be enough. To lump the three of them together in order to create a cohesive concept of the political unconscious would be a mistake. I can thus only state what I have taken from each of them: from Foucault I have taken the idea of the "discursive unconscious" (although he never refers to the disciplinary power of discourse with this term), from Žižek the "symptom," and from Butler the idea of "foreclosure" and "melancholic" return, the double operation of the norm. These interrelated, yet different, forms of subjection (and resistance) make it necessary to interrogate and understand the puzzle of "ideological desire" (the return of desire as a symptom) and its workings as a political unconscious through a series of (violent) effects within the discourse of nationalism.

The difference between Žižek and Butler is particularly telling. Both Žižek and Butler consider the question of desire in relation to power. Both theorize the void in discourse, that surplus which *exceeds* discourse and ideology, pointing to the analytic gap that lies in Žižek's terms between language and desire and in Butler's terms between subjection and subjectivity, a gap that is accessible and intelligible only through specifications, and again only to a degree. I dare say that for both Butler in *The Psychic Life of Power* and Žižek in *The Sublime Object of Ideology*, this gap is the nodal point of their social and political theory. However, it is precisely in the articulation and theorization of this gap that the difference between them emerges: while Žižek, following Lacan, articulates the gap as a deficiency (the lack of the phallus) that is filled with ideological fantasy, Butler articulates it as a loss filled with pain and humiliation. For Žižek, the Real, a surplus of desire, that extra which is unbound by time, narrative, history, and events and which exists irrespective of any external intervention or experience, thus always stays the same, becomes meaningful only through processes of symbolization; for Butler, following Foucault, desire (excluding perhaps the drive for existence) is already a "discursive desire." By contrast, to Žižek that place which exceeds discourse is also a topography of resistance. For Butler, the unknown is already known and a priori has a social "sense." That is, for Butler, to use Derrida's term, foreclosed homosexual desire has a signifiable sense in spite of its absence.

It is these differences but also the similarities between Foucault's, Žižek's, and Butler's critique of domination and power that provide a new possibility for rethinking political reality as a trajectory of history, ideology, and desire. I can now reformulate the question regarding the political unconscious in this way: how does the political unconscious offer, under certain conditions of possibility, a critique of the gap between the visible and the invisible, between reality and desire? Although I dedicate the next few chapters to this question, I want to offer yet some further clarifications regarding the political unconscious.

My aim is not to search for a synthesis between desire and discourse, or to close up the gap between visible and invisible reality. I am not asking how the subject is interpolated into the nation and national society. Rather, my intention is to study how a national discourse institutes a politics of desire manifested as the symptom of hatred; how the subject comes to serve, even when in disbelief, the grandiose illusions of nationalism (national unity, sovereign control, militaristic security, and so on) with devotion and productivity or, to reiterate Butler's question with a twist: How does the subject come to desire the nation?

Given that power always "wants" something, the investigation into dominant hate discourses through the study of desire and its disavowal in speech (for example, the study of forms of idealization),[60] and through national utterances that prohibit desire ("there is no good Arab"), opens up a space for articulating ideological fantasies ("a good Arab is a dead Arab") through which hatred as the symptom of repressed desire manifests itself. If we think of the political unconscious as a psychic apparatus of control intended to protect and reestablish the order of the nation in times of conflict or panic, then the political unconscious should be considered as the "ruse" of discourse. Of course, we should not forget that in the process not all subjects blindly serve the norm. Some come to doubt national politics and develop a self-sacrificial subversive critique. In the gap between ideological desire (the political unconscious) and the subject's courageous self-sacrificial subversion (consciousness of attachment without fear) lies a potential space for a discursive relational change. By that I mean that one cannot resist hatred (death) in the midst of war and violence without re-symbolizing and re-cognizing the necessary and impossible possible, the singular attachment to the other.

The psychic power of discourse, which is the blind spot of discourse, is based in prohibitions and denials. In contrast to formal laws, or attitudes, normative prohibitions operate as speech refusals that protect and defend national discourse ("It's not true; I do not love Arabs").[61] Within such discursive refusals, forms of blame and denial signify the lost desire of the other and constitute and legitimize an ideology of desire. Those who are refused are frequently subjects of hatred, but ipso facto also of unconscious love.[62] The concept of the political unconscious conceived as the unconscious of discourse, the speech that denies itself, opens up a new horizon for theorizing the desire of the other and its effects on national politics, too often ignored or dismissed from politics of nationalism and its violent effects. It draws attention to processes of discursive splitting between the thinkable and the unthinkable, the known unknown which, although it cannot be recognized, can be counteracted by unknotting national politics.

Not all is lost. At certain historical moments, ideological desires can, as Žižek says, be disentangled. The visit by Anwar El-Sadat to Israel in 1977 was such an unraveling, a "working through" event that contrived the possibility for both Arabs and Jews to *feel* for a moment the fantasy which they have known and refused to recognize for many decades. Perhaps the truth and reconciliation committees in South Africa allowed the perpetrators and the victims, even if only for a moment, to regain anew the fantasy of neighborly desire. Such moments rearticulate the power of foreclosed knowledge, allowing for a renewed awakening of desire for life. In a Foucaultian sense, the political unconscious is responsible for the organization of prohibition in language, that which is constituted as knowledge by terms of refusal. What is, however, a refused knowledge (wanting to not know)? Can we say that refused knowledge indicates what one could not have known or what one refused to have known? Is refused knowledge really knowledge?[63]

These questions require collaboration between the sciences of cognition, psychology, philosophy, and history. We can only say for sure that there may be danger in what we do not know, but even more so when we *refuse* to know. Refusing to know is what Žižek defines as a fetishist disavowal: "I know it but I refuse to fully assume the consequences of this knowledge, so that I can continue acting as if I don't know it," or "I know it, but I don't want to know that I know."[64] Such fetishistic disavowal characterized most collective thinking in Nazi Germany. But it is not unique to Nazi Germany. It is unfortunately too often the common "logic" of power, the ruse of hegemonic power. Each day we refuse to know what we know about what is taking place in Gaza or Sudan, the Congo or Somalia, and so on. We see images of genocide, ethnic cleansing, and torture, images of victims of famine, illness, and wars, and to our "shut" eyes they are not only images of "remote places," but our "refused knowledge" of knowing. The refusal to know about the Nazi camps or the Palestinian camps, or about the torture at Guantánamo Bay, is a form of desire "not to know," an ideological desire, which is not merely a self-serving ruse, but a desire to detach one's identity from the other, an unconscious split between one's self and the other to whom we "owe" our love. Or, the other way around, it is a form of narcissism in which when looking in the mirror one sees only the ego without the "I"—the face of the other in front. Refusing to know signifies the unbearable "enigma of the desire of the Other." Charles Mills defines such a refusal as knowledge without seeing.[65]

Wohl argues that the subject's imaginary relations to the conditions of his or her existence are part of the subject's way of confronting the demands of society. Oppressed people often fantasize their rebellion, their freedom, perhaps their revenge. The national discourse of powerful states in war, like Israel or the United Sates, captures fantasies of normalization through logistic and metaphorical speech (revealed by media discussions, historical archives, scholarly works, and military operations) that "erases" the other and disconnects the "enemy" from one's conditions of existence (by keeping the eyes turned forward while raising symbolic and concrete walls).[66] Such fantasies are a clear form of ideological desire built on the ruins of unthinkable love and impossible attachments. In between desire and denial, in this possible-impossible gap, the subject of nationalism is interpolated into the nation through the hatred of the other. Whether we are

Israelis, Congolese, Americans, Sudanese, and so on, national hatred transforms us into a "death machine" when the desire of the other remains refused, denied, and foreclosed in discourse as a symptom of nationalism. How does the political unconscious operate? By what mechanisms are love and hate eclipsed in discourse? The specific mechanisms whereby the political unconscious "shows" itself in language are the focus of the next chapter.

THREE

The Mechanisms of Social Idealization and Splitting

Many who have studied conflict and reconciliation believe in the power of dialogue and discussion between neighbors, communities, or nations as a necessary process toward renouncing violence and ending conflict. Lately scholars have added to their list of recommendations public confessions, such as those before the South African truth and reconciliation commissions, or criminal tribunals as a remedy to violence. Adversaries, say many experts studying reconciliation processes, must open themselves to feelings of hurt and injustice, which through dialogue are reworked collaboratively.[1] Of course, few would argue with collaborative attempts to talk, forgive, and reconcile. While dialogue reflects, at least on its face, a will to resolve the conflict, negotiations often fail not only because the parties have reached a dead end or are unable to agree but also because negotiations reproduce the language that has failed the parties from the very start, because dialogue itself has become a venue for violent language, because dominant groups tend to see dialogue as their privilege and under their authority. If we are not aware of the workings of psychic defenses and their signifiers, if we do not pay attention to psychic barriers in speech, dialogue itself can become a repetition of the unsaid and hence the normalization of violence. Time and time again, reality—in Sudan, Palestine, or Zaire, to name just a few places of conflict—has shown that the road to sustained collaborative effort is paved with repeated failures and transgressions. What are we missing? On the assumption that power struggles tell of pains and pleasures, fears and their denials, what aspect of reality is escaping our theoretical understanding of politics?

In this chapter I look at how defense mechanisms of the political unconscious operate within public speech through the analysis of resistances and fixations in speech, revealing how prejudice and hate speech are reproduced and persist despite the fact that groups often conceive of themselves as liberal, tolerant, pluralistic, progressive, and visibly less segregated or, in other words, show how prejudices and stereotypes remain stubbornly "identitarian" forces.[2] When divided communities engage in prolonged and intractable national or regional conflicts, these repetitive rhetorical schemas become serious invisible hindrances to peace. A particularly strong manifestation of that can be seen in attempts at dialogue that fail when we fail to acknowledge and circumscribe the desire of the other; we fail language and language fails us when prejudices, those modes of dogma, reproduce fixations within dialogue and become barriers to peace. Hence, I focus in this chapter on the politics of (impossible) words, on unaddressed desires in the form of accusations and split language that are, however, unacknowledged in dialogue. Yet speakers speak to "justify their claims with reason" and passionately advance what they believe is true and honest.[3] Dialogue, I propose, moves in at least two spheres: the sphere of claims (for justice, recognition, autonomy, security, etc.), and the sphere of desire, that is, the sphere of possibilities in the realm of the impossible, which is also part of dialogue in absentee. Trying to account for what I want of the other and what the other wants of me is a crucial moment in dialogue and the challenge of prejudice.

After World War II, many social psychologists, shaken by anti-Semitism, racism, and McCarthyism, raised questions about the nature of prejudices and stereotypes. Aronson's vignette in the "Social Animal" depicting a typical anti-Semitic stereotypic conversation is a well-known example. No matter what evidence you adduce against anti-Semitism, the anti-Semite will always find justification and proof of his or her logic. Similarly, a dialogue between a racist and an anti-racist will always be simultaneously circular and parallel, reflecting the individual's subjective loyalty to his or her group. This inaccessible circularity of difference shows the power of interpellation to the group, what Derrida would perhaps call the politics of the *differance*.

Psychoanalytic studies have emphasized the power of psychic barriers that fixate and fetishize unresolved, repressed psychic traumas. Works on trauma and post-trauma are extensively cited in studies on the hindrances to reconciliation. These studies show how fear, anger, and mistrust, as in the case of unresolved and untreated past trauma, not only impede cooperative relations between communities but also produce new antagonisms and hatred, how trauma reconstitutes prejudices, and how psychological obstacles in general "are often fatal, leading to new sources of hate and thus to new forms of conflict."[4] Noelle McAfee in her book *Democracy and the Political Unconscious* boldly hypothesizes that the modern nation-state can be viewed, at least in part, as the product of defense mechanisms such as repression, reaction-formation, isolation, and projection. "Could defenses against modernity's traumas," she asks, "have had such power and made possible the necessary coalitions and coalescences?"[5] In McAfee's view, public trauma, particularly repressed public trauma (for example, the urgency to get back to normal life after 9/11), should be considered as a collective experience which is key to the understanding of wars as a repetitive-compulsive phenomenon that reenacts the return of the repressed again and again.

Even if we do not frame national conflict within interpretations of past trauma events, we can say that hatred works within the bounds of language that is not itself, and that politics reconstructs the unsaid by other means. In this vein, I wish to call attention to the workings of two *psychic mechanisms*—idealization and splitting—that operate as defensive forces to protect communal beliefs and prejudices, those sine qua non assumptions as knowledge, which when challenged or refuted create more distress than the thing itself. The assumption-knowledge-belief that the other is radically bad and apt to destroy "me," this already organized mental structure which becomes part of the self, must, in order to be constructive and protective, reproduce itself time and again within national culture, identity, and politics. My aim is to show how psychic resistance to the desire of the other (to peace) can operate within language as ideology and hindrance even in the midst of dialogue for peace, as if untouched by dialogue, or in spite of it, and how psychic defenses operate to protect hate discourse that re-creates conflict as the status quo.[6]

This chapter, therefore, is a preliminary effort to study two psychic mechanisms—idealization and splitting—and their effects on the dialogue between two conflict groups. I will show how these two psychic forces implicitly dominate the dialogical process and allow old prejudices to reappear in speech, and how prejudices and stereotypes can be reconstructed and repeated under the guise of dialogue when desire is veiled from the politics of the conflict.

Let me take, as an example, one scene that depicts many from a Jewish-Palestinian dialogue group to facilitate a better understanding of the dominant obstacles hindering Jewish-Palestinian mutual recognition.[7] The example demonstrates how speech can become a substitute for disavowed, unthought language, how interpellated speech can be reproduced in dialogue. There are of course numerous issues at play in such groups and different interactive stages, including moments of cooperation and solidarity.[8] My reading is focused on dialogical moments that were pregnant with (unnamed) desires, obsessive repetitions, circumvolutions, and hidden signifiers. This reading shifts the focus to those mechanisms that protect subjective speech. Or, differently put, I show how (national) ideology is reenacted and instituted as subjective speech in public through the workings of the political unconscious as I have defined it in Chapter 2, discarding the significance of that possible-impossible of speech.

Let me, then, open with a short exchange between a by-national group of Israeli-Palestinians and Israeli-Jewish students. The speech event took place during the second meeting. After a long silence and feelings of embarrassment, an Israeli-Jewish woman turns to the facilitators (a Palestinian man and a Jewish woman) and says:

> "Do you expect us to speak freely?"
> "We want to understand what's going on," replies the Palestinian facilitator.
> Silence. . . .
> ISRAELI-JEWISH MAN: "My reaction to the workshop? The fact that we came to this meeting says something already. The group is not a representative sample from the educational point of view."
> ISRAELI-JEWISH WOMAN: "In the introductory role-playing everything was well and good, but if we are going to bring up some problems, disagreement will follow for sure."

"Yes, but we are not a representative sample," the man insists.
Another Israeli-Jewish woman intervenes: "The question is: what's the purpose of the workshop? The purpose is not to be a representative sample, but to examine the processes between two peoples."
After a few exchanges between the Israeli-Jewish students, an Israeli-Palestinian woman briefly interrupts the Jewish-dominated discussion and says: "I disagree with you," turning to the Jewish man.
But he insists: "Not everyone in our society would agree to come to these kinds of meetings."
This goes on for quite some time until the Palestinian facilitator finally stops the discussion by reflecting: "The discussion is taking place only between the Jewish students."

From the very first moment, the Jewish students framed the bi-national dialogue group as a unique and special event which did not represent reality. The Jewish students (who spoke) viewed it as a "gathering of goodwill" and a special opportunity to meet Palestinians who live in Israel in order to *learn them*, which, as the playwright Rebecca Gilman says in *Spinning into Butter*, is "no different than hating them." The Palestinians on their part saw the meetings mainly as an opportunity to voice their inequality, suffering and injuries under Israel's discriminatory treatment of its non-Jewish citizens. Dominated groups know all about their oppressors; they have no need to learn them.[9]

In the first few sessions, some of the Jewish participants insisted on defining the Palestinians in the group as a singular and ideal group: educated, liberal, and moderate. A Jewish woman said: "I think that the Arabs in this group are trying to assimilate and are not quite representative . . . they are intellectuals, educated, and in general they have a very rich culture of their own." A racist comment in itself, this definition excludes and reconstitutes the Palestinian group as an "ideal other"—educated, funny, and nice. What does this idealization signify, and what stands behind the fantasy of a "good enemy"?

In a manner typical of exclusionary (racist) thinking, the Jewish insistence on the uniqueness of the Palestinian group is somewhat similar to what Simon Clarke describes in relation to the British perception of themselves in contrast to others: " 'We' British nation are tolerant, 'we' open our arms to you, but in doing so the 'we' marginalize 'you.' "[10] Similarly, Sara

Ahmed examines the ways multiculturalism involves stranger fetishism. She writes: "The act of welcoming 'the stranger' as the origin of difference produces the very figure of 'the stranger' as the one who can be taken in." Hence she argues that "othering can take place by acts of inclusion within multicultural discourse."[11] Idealization of Arabs by the Jewish group can be seen in similar ways: "we," that is, the "good Jews," are willing to talk to you and include you as long as "you" are nice, compliant, and good. Until the First Intifada (the Palestinian uprising) in 1987, the Arabs in Israel were indeed conceived by many Israelis (and certainly by the state) as the possible good other-stranger-enemy.

The mechanism of idealization operates as a defense against the failure to perceive reality accurately.[12] But from my point of view, the problem is not necessarily a question of accuracy of perception and judgment. Rather, following Freud, idealization is about remodeling reality, changing the relation to others and the world in ways that fit into the psychic schema of threat through strategies of denial, that is, marking the Other as different and distant. In contrast to the popular meaning of idealization, idealization in psychoanalysis reflects a narcissistic arrogance, a phantasmal need, an illusory creation of the other as unequal. The target of analysis here is not the idealized, but the idealizer who through the process of idealization gains control over his or her feared desires and prohibited relations by turning ambivalent desire into fiction, into an ideal that eliminates the bad object of desire. But to what purpose? By asking this question, we must remember that in dialogic situations the dominant group always strives to present itself as human, moral, and liked, to be recognized as just and be desired by the other. The desire of the other is the dominant group's guarantee of power, self-righteousness, and the joy of ruling. "If we are liked then we must be good and just." Even the Nazis, at least at the beginning, strived to show the world their "good" face, their humanity and civilized moral-legal behavior. Wasn't Tresinstadt a sign of that desire to appear human and civilized to the outside world? By isolating the dialogical group from reality (we, the group, are different from the rest of the other Jews and Arabs), the Jewish group assures that they can love and be loved *if* only the Arabs will be good and loyal.

Returning to the dialogic example, I want to point out how the Jewish group appeals to the Palestinians to give up their extreme demands and let them be loved:

JEWISH WOMAN: "Each side is stuck. Perhaps I should say that I'm willing to give up a little of my power. But I'll only do it if the other side will be willing too."

FACILITATOR: "Would you be willing to give up your power without conditions?"

PALESTINIAN WOMAN: "They want both the land and peace and in the end they will throw me a little something."

PALESTINIAN WOMAN: "They are not willing to concede on things I want."

JEWISH WOMAN: "I am willing to concede."

ANOTHER JEWISH WOMAN: "*You* are not willing to concede anything; you will not lend yourself to openness."

PALESTINIAN WOMAN: "You told me your opinion—I want a Palestinian state."

JEWISH WOMAN: "It is necessary to move in stages, not in a single step."

PALESTINIAN WOMAN: "The things you said you are willing to give me are not enough."

JEWISH WOMAN: "What would satisfy you?"

ANOTHER JEWISH WOMAN: "Why do you need the land?"

In other words, the Jewish women are asking about desire: What is it that the Palestinian women desire? How can we, the Jews, satisfy that desire? And how can we, the Jews, be desired by you, the Palestinians? The Palestinian students, however, refuse to live up to the Jewish fantasy. They express their resentment at the normalized relations under domination and the humiliating circumstances of the occupation; they are unwilling to mask their pain, or to tell their story as an ordinary narrative of suffering equal to the suffering of the Jewish students. They refuse to be the "nice" Other, to express gratitude for the right to be included in the Jewish state, or to be idealized.[13]

By idealizing and fictionalizing the Palestinians, the Jews appropriate the Palestinians as familiar objects of control. At the same time, though, idealization is also a response to panic and prohibition, a response to the possible-impossible, a disavowal of that which is most frightening, turning the other into an obsession. It was Freud who pointed to the double nature of idealization and its power to split love from hate, glorification from disparagement, by disavowing the real. He writes: "Indeed, as we found in the origin of the fetish, it is possible for the original instinct-presentation to be split into two, one part undergoing repression, while the remainder, just on account of its intimate association with the other, undergoes idealization."[14] Freud's quote further suggests that idealization constitutes a fetishized world of ideas and objects. I will return to fetish ideas, but there is another issue concerning idealization that must be discussed beforehand in order to understand how prejudice and stereotypes are perpetuated within dialogue. This discussion of idealization, as Freud's quote shows, cannot be complete without the concept of splitting. How does splitting work?

Splitting of the object,[15] like idealization, is a psychic defense mechanism that protects the subject's world from collapsing.[16] Freudian splitting identifies a cultural and sexual system of (normative) prohibitions that constitutes the desire of the (forbidden) other as a threat. Klein takes the notion of splitting between the "bad" and "good" object a step further, speaking of splitting as a regulatory mechanism to repress and mask the desire of the other (or parts of the other). As Klein writes: "The mechanism of splitting the imagos is important; the ego turns away from the object that threatens danger, but it turns towards the friendly object in an attempt to repair the imaginary injuries it has inflicted."[17] Following her concept but framing it in a different language, one can say that splitting works as a contrived blindness to that which has already been recognized but nonetheless disavowed. The same threatening other is split into both a bad and hated and a loved and admired object. Despite Klein's drive-related conceptualization of desire, her object-related psychoanalysis brings feelings of injury, danger, and threat into the field of the other and into the social world of imagined relations. In her theory, the fantasy of the other constitutes a social world dominated by love and hate. If the other is perceived as bad only (since the good is disavowed), reality too is imagined as persecutory and dangerous.

In an attempt to hold on to the image of the idealized (good, submissive) Arab as a source of pleasure and self-aggrandizement ("*we* are good because we accept *you*"), yet at the same time facing an unsettled reality (the Palestinians refuse to be invisible), Jewish discourse becomes split: The "good Arab" is abstracted—cut off—and denied from language ("there is no such thing as a good Arab"). It becomes a fictitious configuration, a figment of denied imagination which nonetheless continues to take part in the political reality of national discourse within the configuration of the bad other as a wish without a language.

Moreover, as the Jewish students are frustrated in their determination to ascertain what the Palestinians "really" want, the reality of the conflict invades the room in full force with the usual accusations and justifications that mirror the common expressions and terminologies in Israel's public domain. The two national groups engage in passionate and stormy disputation, fiercely debating issues such as who is more moral or civilized, who is the greater victim, and who is willing or not to make concessions for peace; the land becomes a signifier of identity and the target of harsh animosity and disagreement, as does the law of return for Palestinians who were expelled in 1948. The two sides quarrel over inequality, discrimination, and the Palestinians' stories of persecution, daily harassment, and humiliation, and they share their mutual fears.[18] When the Palestinian participants push hard, describing painful and humiliating situations, accusing the Jewish students as a group of not being really ready for peace, contending that Israel can never be democratic as a Jewish state, and demanding their stolen land back, a dramatic shift takes place in the atmosphere and in discourse: the good, educated, smart, pleasant Arab turns into the "bad," "dangerous" Arab. At this stage, the Jewish participants resort to a familiar and common rhetorical tactic of colonizers: they repeatedly demand that the Palestinians declare their loyalty to the State of Israel and denounce terrorism and suicide bombings:

> JEWISH WOMAN: "[In your culture] a man who kills Jews and then commits suicide is considered a martyr."
> ANOTHER JEWISH WOMAN: "In our religion human lives are sacred."
> PALESTINIAN WOMAN: "The Palestinians in the Occupied Territories witness terrible things. Why should they want to live? What do they have left?"
> JEWISH WOMAN: "We denounced Baruch Goldstein" (Goldstein massacred twenty-nine Palestinians near the Tombs of the Patriarchs in Hebron in 1994).
> PALESTINIAN MAN: "I am also against killings."
> JEWISH WOMAN: "You gave explanations saying that they [the Palestinians] have a reason to murder innocent Jews and you have shown you identify with that, saying you were willing to accept it because you understand them. I am unwilling to accept terrorism from any side, so what you are saying is very irritating."
> PALESTINIAN WOMAN: "I do not support terrorism; I am trying to understand where it comes from."

JEWISH WOMAN: "I want to hear you denounce terrorism out loud; I want you to condemn killings!"

PALESTINIAN WOMAN: "I understand why they did it [referring to a specific incident], though I don't agree with such things."

JEWISH WOMAN: "But what did you feel? When I saw what Baruch Goldstein did, I was SHO-CKED. How did *you* feel?" (The latter is in reference to an incident where Jews were killed.)

PALESTINIAN WOMAN: "I was shocked too; when I saw the killing of a female Jewish soldier, I almost cried."

JEWISH WOMAN, ON THE ATTACK: "By the way you say it, I can't see that you are really shocked."

PALESTINIAN WOMAN, NOT BACKING DOWN: "When I see babies dying in Serbia and Africa I cry too."

JEWISH WOMAN, IN ANGER: "You are trying to strike a balance; you see both sides and soften the picture."

At some point the Palestinian participants counterattack: "We've said that we are against terrorism many times," "You hear what you want to hear," "We say what we believe in," "I don't want you to give me the feeling that we are the bad guys and you are the good guys," or "Enough, I don't have to denounce terrorism at every meeting." The battle goes on for many sessions. No matter how many times the Palestinian participants say, "I understand the killings and suicide bombings, but I disagree with such things," the Jewish group continues to push hard, demanding that each and every one of them preface his or her speech with a condemnation of terrorism and actually show remorse. But the Palestinians refuse to speak under rules that say "Condemn terrorism first, talk later," and harden their line.

That moment of change in discourse (the erasure of the "good" Arab from speech) represents an escalated phase of symbolic control in language; what went on in the group represents the power relations outside. The Jewish students' responsiveness to compliance and objection to resistance, the change in their approach to the Palestinian group from patronized inclusiveness to separation, reproduce the tactics of the state and its governing modes of control. Neve Gordon identifies two transformative moments in Israel's relations with the Palestinians in the Occupied Territories (which, of course, projects on Israeli-Palestinians and reconstructs the Jewish-Israeli consciousness and logic as well).[19] During the first two decades of the Occupation, Israel, says Gordon, exercised a variety of monitoring mechanisms, counting, checking, registering, examining, inspecting, and scrutinizing the Palestinians' daily lives, but overall Israel did attempt to secure the well-being of the population and to normalize the occupation. Facilitating the compliance of the Palestinian inhabitants (through economic, health care, educational, and agricultural programs), Israel did its best "to constitute them as subjects of the occupying power."[20] After 2000 (the second intifada), though, a dramatic shift of emphasis took place. When Israel learned that it could not suppress Palestinian nationalism, it stopped caring for the population and focused on maintaining resources, without any responsibility for people. Gordon writes: "If before the second uprising Israel tried to avoid killing Palestinians, from September 2000 the finger pulling the trigger confronted fewer obstacles ... [and] ... a politics of death slowly emerged."[21]

My point is that the observable shift in language in the group from the "good" to the "bad" Arab, thereby imposing barriers on Palestinian free speech, mirrors the transformation in reality from disciplinary control to sovereign power and separation. After the first few initial sessions, when the Jewish group came to realize that they could not control the Palestinians' determination to tell their story and could not enforce their imaginary picture of unity (without equality) and "love" (the Palestinians' love), the Jewish students "reorganized" around the substitute tactic of demanding loyalty and imposing separation.[22]

The rhetoric of loyalty and betrayal signifies the sine qua non of disavowed language. The demand for loyalty circulates like a code for and measure of the vanishing "good" Arabs; it casts a palimpsestic image of the "good" Arab which has been erased and yet is still very much in the room, plainly apparent in the demand for the loyalty of the other. The discourse of loyalty (and betrayal) signifies the failure of identification with both the good-compliant Arab (in the register of the unconscious imaginary, the field of desire) and the bad Arab (in the register of the symbolic, the field of spoken language). In such impossible situations, "our reality can be real only if the real outside reality is negated, attributed to the Other who somehow stole it from us."[23] This means that the Jewish group must find a way to recognize their hate as a counter-discourse to the lost love of the Israeli Palestinians, who the Jews feel have "robbed" them of the pleasure of domination and of the illusion of their moral superiority by denying them the measure of love as compliance. Hate is produced not because the other is perceived as "bad" or threatening, but because the other will not give to us the gift of being "good" enough. When I try to understand why there is such an obsessive emphasis on Palestinian loyalty in the group (but also in Israeli politics), I cannot ignore my feeling that the Jewish group harbors a great anxiety that cannot be represented, but that nonetheless seeks representation, and that in between idealization on the one hand and demands for loyalty on the other, a language of hate is formed as the nodal point of the relations. [24]

Listen to the panic and the way in which demands for loyalty substitute for desire:

> JEWISH WOMAN: "I want to talk about the issue of loyalty—you live in this country and you claim that you do not have equal rights. But on the other hand when we talk about the army, which is part of the State and loyalty to the State. . . . If you expect to receive rights you should also have duties."
>
> PALESTINIAN WOMAN: "The Druze serve in the army, and what do they get?"
>
> JEWISH WOMAN: "Your approach tells me that you have a poor view of soldiers. In my view it is a question of give and take. In order for me to believe you, you should show that you care and that you are willing to take responsibility."
>
> PALESTINIAN MAN: "What is loyalty for you?"
>
> "To serve in the army," replies the Jewish woman.
>
> PALESTINIAN WOMAN: "Over my dead body! What, to fight against my brothers? No way!"
>
> PALESTINIAN MAN (IGNORING THE PALESTINIAN WOMAN'S OUTBURST AND PRESSING THE QUESTION): "Loyalty from the security point of view, or juristically?"
>
> PALESTINIAN WOMAN: "Even in the army you do not give equal rights to the Druze."
>
> JEWISH WOMAN: "Well, I think we try to see you as one group and not divide you into different segments; you are all Arabs."
>
> PALESTINIAN MAN: "I do not think that you are loyal to me as a citizen of the Israeli state, because you are the superior and I am the inferior."
>
> JEWISH WOMAN: "Your self-defense is a threat to us. We do not define [loyalty] in the same way. Every evil done to you is our survival."

Demands for loyalty (hence accusations of betrayal) frame the Other as the abject "bad object," taking the other's loyalty to the limits of impossibility: The Other can never be loyal enough. Even when the Palestinians assure the Jewish group that the problem is not the fidelity or infidelity of the Arabs in Israel (for Israel is their state as well), but rather the nature of their inclusion in the state, to the Jews the Palestinians "cannot be loyal." This shadow-theater, or metapolitics, to use Žižek's term, is what I call a split discourse between the good and bad enemy, a mirror of mirrors in the reality of love and hate. In this brief exchange, as in longer ones, a meta-language of "ifs"—"if only you were good" . . . "if you just loved us enough" . . . "*if* . . ."—assumes its presence through an inverse dialogue of loyalty and betrayal. The Jewish talk gets obsessively wrapped up in the conditional mode of "if," which becomes the signifier of desire. In other words, here we see how, through idealization and splitting, psychic operations work within particular utterances forming national discourse.

How do we account for splitting in politics? Is splitting always political? Can splitting not be political? Put differently, how are hate and prejudice reinstated as the regular of speech even during attempts at dialogue? The obsessive demand for loyalty shows not only the limits of speech (because the profession of loyalty will never be enough) but also the power of psychic mechanisms to produce a substitute language—a counter-language—that hides desire in the form of demands for loyalty signifying hate speech. The desire to be loved by the other (love that creates our self-esteem) is what, I suggest, parties in conflict tend to deny and reject as unthinkable.[25] Given that one cannot demand or master the desire of the Other, but only demand the other's compliance, conflict opens a space for the "absence itself."[26] Splitting, "[this] very tricky, hyperactive word that is loaded with aggressive fantasies and thoughts of disaster,"[27] allows for the transformation of the "good other" into the imponderable other as enemy, the enemy who emerges from the good as the bad beyond measure.

When the other becomes an "absolute enemy," dialogue enters into the realm of religion; the "bad" becomes the bad of all times, from Pharaoh to Titus to Hitler to Arafat and to the rest of the Palestinians. The collapse of time brings to life traumatic events that occurred centuries ago "as though they had occurred the day before."[28] From this point on, it is evil itself that comes to rule reality as a schema, while discourse comes to be regulated and regular more and more by defenses and by fantasies of disaster surpassing the limits of the known, logical, normative, and historical. The Jewish national discourse, even its liberal wing, cannot accommodate the "ungrammatically" speaking other—the noncompliant other—without fear of being consumed by the "monstrous Other."

During a discussion on why the Arabs who live in Israel have to call themselves Palestinians, one Jewish woman said: "The definition of 'Palestinian' is very loaded. It feels as if there is a monster that is going to eat us slowly, slowly."

FACILITATOR: "Why does it bother you that he (the Palestinian speaker) calls himself a Palestinian?"

The discussion goes on for quite some time until a Jewish woman makes the following comment: "It is interesting that when Ilana (the Jewish woman) said that for her a Palestinian is a monster that will eat us slowly, no one felt a need to respond."

Still no one responds.

Such speech is doubly problematic, not only because there is a schema of the absolute enemy-monster, but because the "bad" other is phantasmagorically cut off and separated from the "good subject." Of course it is not easy to imagine the good and the bad at once, or to associate hatred with desire for love in the same thought. Poets and artists have done it better than scientists. Yet, hatred and love combined is precisely where politics unconsciously touches on issues of the Real; on separation and closeness, inclusion and exclusion, war and peace.

Taking Klein's politics of fantasy a step further again, I argue that in intractable conflicts, peace becomes fetishized. A fetishist concept of peace both renounces and idealizes peace at the same time. Such terms as "real peace," "just peace," "true peace," and "total peace" are examples of violent, fetishist concepts of peace. These concepts of total or true peace "push our desire beyond proper limits, transforming it into a 'desire that contains the infinite,' elevating it into an absolute striving that cannot ever be satisfied."[29] A *New York Times* reporter summarized his interview with Israel's 16th Defense Minister Shaul Mofaz (17 September 2008) as follows: "He (Mofaz) has also described the negotiations with the Palestinians as a waste of time although he says he is committed to making peace with them." Such unconscious double language (or splitting)—being committed to peace and denying its possibility at the same time—establishes a notion of unrealizable peace, a peace that is only to be hoped for. It is a language of peace that constitutes violent and unthinkable relations. Mr. Mofaz is not upset by the impossibility of peace (after all, he can still remain committed to it), but by the waste of time entailed necessary for possible peace. In many peace dialogues what is truly feared is peace itself.[30]

Wars are indeed devastating and painful, but they are also familiar. Peace, on the other hand, like love, can only be imagined, perhaps as another war. In the Jewish-Palestinian peace dialogues, loyalty and betrayal are what a "waste of time" is for Mr. Mofaz—the veiled demand for the compliance and submission of the "good Arab." These signs fill the gaps between saying (we are committed to peace), desire (the desire for the Other), and acting (in violence), and present a substitute language to avoid the fear of peace, the fear of including the outsider other inside. Similarly, accusations of ungratefulness substitute for unnamable desire, for love that the Jews will not admit and the Palestinians, like a stern (phallic?) mother, will not give.[31] The other side of this coin, the fear to include the other inside, is also the fear of dependency. To this discussion I turn in Chapter 4.

The Lure of Proximity and the Fear of Dependency

The response of hatred in reaction to a hidden fear of personal and collective dependency is perhaps intuitive yet not obvious. In psychoanalysis the connections between dependency and hatred is a common idea recognized as part of the oedipal drama of development. The dependency of the child on the parents and the dependency between the therapist and the patient in transference and counter-transference are only a couple of examples. Lacan underscores the dependency of the subject on the (impossible) desire of the Other as a primary factor constituting the subject's psychic structure. In his interpretation of Hamlet's desire (to his mother) it becomes clear that Hamlet's dependency on the desire for the (m)other, yet its impossibility, turns into an obsession and cruelty toward Ophelia, signifying this impossibility.[1] But, as I said, the concept of dependency functioning on the level of group hatred requires a further conceptualization beyond individual dependency. How should we understand the working of dependency (and its disavowal) within the social field? And how does the language of hatred signify that dependency which we lure and fear? To answer these questions, I will, however, start my exploration with a personal note.

My father never forgave the Germans. For many years, as a child and an adolescent, I was not allowed to use products made in Germany. He himself refused German monetary compensation. Over dinner one night, I asked him if he *still* hated the Germans, assuming that as a Holocaust survivor he must have hated them for some time. "I never hated them *there* . . . and I don't hate them now," he said somberly. Like many survivors, my father rarely used the names Auschwitz or Buchenwald or Teresienstadt (the camps he was held in).[2] All his stories about the camps would start with a pause, then he'd take a big breath of air and begin: "*There* . . . we were too weak to hate, so *now* we should give *them* the pleasure of being hated?" What does it mean to refuse to give someone the pleasure of being hated? What do you give (or take) when you hate? It was hard for me then, as a young woman, to not be skeptical. But over the years, both in private and in public, I kept hearing similar statements from other survivors. Why would my father not give the Germans the "pleasure" of being hated? Why did he refuse to "enjoy" a "good" hate?

Primo Levi was once asked why there are no expressions of hate in his writing, why there is no desire for revenge: "Have you forgiven them?"[3] His answer was "No, I have not forgiven any of the culprits, nor am I willing to forgive a single one of them." Yet Levi refused to hate the Nazis. As a witness to and victim of horrors, he speaks with reason and great detachment. Using reason, he claimed, never let him cultivate hatred, or a desire for revenge. Like many of his interviewers over the years, but perhaps for other reasons, I remain skeptical to the fact that reason alone can preclude hatred. Levi also said: "Even less do I accept hatred as directed collectively at an ethnic group, for example, all the Germans; if I accepted it, I would feel that I was following the precepts of Nazism, which was founded precisely on national and racial hatred." Is there some kind of clue here?[4] Was my father echoing Levi's "logic"? And what "logic" would that be—of war, of protection, or of a detachment that already signifies an anxious attachment? Can Levi help us see the concept of hatred in a new way? Was Levi struggling (in the name of reason) against attachment not only to memories that haunted him all his life, but to his perpetrators, the objects of his hate, the Nazis themselves, an attachment (preserved in the ego) which I suppose made his ethical project of writing so difficult? Levi (like my father) was a victim of war. I suppose that he, as a victim, "knew" the violent force of attachment to the perpetrator and the bondage of hatred, even though he did not admit it in such unordinary terms. Was his insistent refusal to hate, something he repeated in almost every interview, a declaration of disengagement, a struggle to distance himself from hatred, the instrument of the perpetrator, to rational non-hatred, in order to veil fears of attachment?

Victims of persecution, colonization, and subjugation know their dependency all too well. Although not all systems of subjection produce a similar apparatus of dependency, excluded subjects are usually redefined through their dependency on the very system that excludes them. What do I mean by dependency, and in what ways are dependency and attachment internal to each other in systems of control and desire? The Palestinians, for example, live this dependency minute by minute. Israel, using technologies of bio-power and techniques of surveillance, has built such a vast and widespread system of control in the West Bank and Gaza that the Palestinian population has become utterly dependent on Israel for survival.[5] The Palestinians do not need evidence of their dependency; their subjugation and forced compliance, the "abnormality" of their lives, speak for themselves and are not part of a hidden reality. They experience the conditions of their oppression directly. They see and feel it through their bodies, in their homes, without relief. Israeli administrative coercion and military power are familiar to them. For the Palestinian people (particularly, but not only, in the West Bank and Gaza Strip), proximity is blocked, walled, barricaded, and fenced. Yet proximity remains a fundamental condition of their subjugation. This is not to say that the Palestinians have no independent life external to Israeli occupation and control. Even under the bleakest terms of surveillance and despite their many difficulties, the Palestinians nonetheless are able to manage political resistance, organize, and continue with schooling, music, and intellectual production. Under such circumstances of oppression, people fight primarily against the conditions of their dependency, not dependency itself. There should not be any contradiction in understanding the transitivity of the self through relations of colonial hybridity, the fact that all identities within systems of difference (Israeli and Palestinian alike) are relational and fighting against the conditions of dependency within terms of oppression.

In contrast to the Palestinians, who cannot escape the awareness of their dependency on Israeli rule, Israel, a sovereign state, has come to believe that by force and tight control it will be able to limit unnecessary contacts and maintain a spatial and relational separation from the Palestinians. This misrecognition, or denial of the Israelis' internal dependency on Palestinian recognition and forms of address, produces a delusional sense of power that is blind to the necessary and fundamental contingency between Israel and its Palestinian-Other. Instead, discourses of mistrust and blame create a psychic segregation from anxieties of influence and inconceivable dependency. If there are fears of dependency, they are silenced and replaced through practices of surveillance and separation: building walls, limiting the movement of the Palestinians, legally preventing Israeli-Palestinians from buying land or expanding their villages.

I am not talking here about, for example, Israel's dependency on Palestinian labor during the 1980s. Rather, my focus is on relations with a "you" which Butler defines as "an other who is interiorized in ways for which I can give no account," yet in geopolitical zones of conflict this "you" becomes the other and the object of an opaque interiorization that constitutes unconscious anxiety and violence to counteract and contain a necessary but impossible account of "you-and-me." The Israeli case demonstrates that the more nations build protective walls around themselves, the more obsessive and illusory separation becomes. Does the building of apparatuses of exclusion and detachment not demonstrate that distancing has not been achieved? That is the paradoxical nature of dependency and its strings of attachment.

A few words on "the necessary" are due here: the structure of the necessary is, according to Laclau and Mouffe, a system of relations between different elements. The idea entails recognizing that all relations have a necessary character. Following the Saussurean concept of language, Laclau and Mouffe conclude that a system is an arrangements of parts in a structure "which transcends and explains its elements."[6] Changes within one element modify the whole. This holds true within unequal power relations as well.[7] Grinberg's historical depiction of Israeli-Palestinian relations delineates exactly such a necessity in which internal changes within Israeli society condition the internality of changes within the Palestinian society. The concept of the necessary, however, does not mean a fixed contingency.

"Necessity [write Laclau and Mouffe] only exists as a partial limitation of the field of contingency."[8] In a similar way, the state of necessity is also the foundation of the exception within the structure of the necessary (an issue to which I will return in my discussion of friendship). At the same time, without articulating the power of *the necessary*—the hidden narrative of subjectivation, politics, and literal existence—it is hard to understand the libidinal intensity and passion that characterize intractable conflicts and hate relations. Without articulating the terms of dependency (its necessity and historical inevitability), we cannot give a "full" (or rather intelligible) account of the intervening elements that produce and shape the specificity of the relations and practices of genocide and other atrocities of hatred.[9] To understand that logic, we have to look closely at the underlying role of dependency in relations of difference and abjection, to understand what makes dependency necessary and refused in tandem.

The relations and conditions of subjective dependency (in contrast to objective servitude and oppression)—such as those that subsisted between the Germans and the Jews, the Young Turks and the Armenians, the Hutu and the Tutsi, and the Serbs and the Croats and that now subsist between Israeli Jews and the Palestinians—are mostly signified relations evident mainly through their effects, including reversals: closeness becomes separation and alienation, intimacy becomes a threat, truth becomes a lie, and so on. These reversals, I argue, are the product of relations of desire, which are always posited as something that is lost but still claims its symbolic appearance, presses charges. In that sense, the idea that one must love the enemy seems fictional, even sacrilegious, yet within the articulation of the terms of dependency it is a necessary idea, necessary precisely because it is prohibited, and like all prohibitions it "makes us believe that what is impossible really exists and [it] is possible for us to encounter it again."[10] Undoubtedly to think about love of the enemy after the Holocaust may spark outrage, yet it is the prevailing discourse of hatred that demands this suspicion, rather than the possibility of love itself. I am not surprised to find so many Holocaust survivors that insist on not hating the Nazis in order not to love.

Hence, against the tradition of modern Western psychology, I contend that the opposite of dependency is not independence and autonomy, as often thought and assumed, but rather isolation and alienation. Relations of independence are already a relation in-dependence and in contingency. One cannot be independent without being *in* dependent relations. Dependence and independence—concepts of difference within the Same—create a field of contingency, the terrain of the social, of exteriority and interiority of practice. To separate dependence and independence as two contradictory concepts already represents a specific social and scientific narrative, determined by the level of modern anxiety that the thought and state of dependency arouses. A subject (person or state) threatened by possible and necessary dependence on another who is the Other to the self, will surely attempt to maintain (even if unconsciously) a physical, spatial and mental separation in order to internally and externally isolate the other and create a sense of disengagement. But, this sense of separation is of course illusory; as disparting and excluding the other does not erase the ontological or the political necessity of dependency. Paradoxically, dependency is restored through its denial, yet giving the subject a sense of power and control which illusion often creates.

It is important to note that I am not attempting to linguistically deconstruct the concept of dependency or to study its genealogical conceptual history. Likewise, I do not claim to be able to identify the moment in which dependency became a developmental problem in modern discourse, indicative of immature human relations bearing negative connotations, particularly in political thought and psychological theory. Still, a few words on the meaning of dependency ought to be said here: Since the nineteenth century, with the psychologization of the individual and the birth of the modern self,[11] dependency has been ambivalently conceived: necessary yet regressive, natural yet pathological, pleasurable yet morally degenerative. Relations of dependency were racialized and gendered by attributing to women and blacks an insufficient maturity, by comparing them to needy children, subordinate and incapable of self-governance and self-reliance. Against the concept of autonomy and self-reliance, dependency is seen at best as "softness" of the self and, in extreme cases, as a pathological loss of the ego's boundaries.[12]

During the 1960s and the 1970s, the social value of dependency became an issue of philosophical and scientific debate. Some believed that the principle of dependency, understood as an affiliation with and care for others, could liberate society from violence and domination.[13] Others argued against

dependency as a form of digression from autonomy and self-rule. Most social scientists see dependency as an inevitable limitation of human existence;
a newborn baby could not survive without the care and attendance of his
or her parents. However, from the baby's moment of birth and onward, the
struggle against dependency is conceived as the task of individuation and
socialization in order to constitute the boundaries and value of the self. In
the modern sciences, autonomy has become the sine qua non of adulthood,
maturity, normalcy, productivity, and personal health.[14] It is not surprising
that in a multicultural society an inevitable dependency of identities is particularly intolerable and abhorrent to dominant groups who see themselves
as influencing but not being influenced, as ruling but not possibly deferring
to the other. Psychoanalytic theory suggests that a denial signified through
violence and hate operates as a defense mechanism to counteract an "unthinkable" and threatening situation. The fear of dependency and its violent effects are particularly evident in power relations of conflict and
hatred. (Do groups go to war to fight against their fear of dependency, to
de-attach from the other who is simultaneously too close and too different?)
My purpose is therefore twofold: to study the fear of dependency and to
discuss the social and political consequences of that fear. I claim that misrecognition of dependency can turn into a discourse of hatred and that this
language of violence splits the consciousness of contingency, masking the
fears of dependency and its unthought desire. I further argue that denied
dependency must be unveiled and recognized through a discourse of the
necessary, not in order to liberate the subject from dependency (as in therapeutic relations), but, by contrast, to transform the fear of dependency into
a language of peace.

Perhaps the most complicated relations to theorize are those silenced
and denied ties outside of the direct symbolization of human interaction
that affect and shape the social field. Hate relations become a problem not
only when hate speech is public but also when certain forms of attachment
and desire are suppressed but do not vanish, when invisible exchanges are at
work and unspoken fears continue to govern discourse and the existing political order. On what basis does denied dependency (attachment, desire)
resemble hatred? Under what conditions does love resemble hatred—not
because love, as many researchers have already noted, can turn into hatred
or vice versa, but because, as some psychoanalysts have noted, "there is no

hate without love"? But when this psychic equivalence of love and hate crosses into the social field, it acquires the characteristics of paradoxes, opposites, reverse rhetoric, surface differences, or diverse techniques of control. To understand this crossing and transformation, to rediscover the contingencies between love and hate in group conflict, to sort, isolate, and regroup the web of "necessary but impossible" relations, we must look more closely at relations of domination and dependency. No doubt "there is nothing more tentative . . . than the process of establishing an order among things," Foucault warns us.[15] With this awareness and caveat in mind, I now turn to unveiling the hidden, underlying connections between domination, dependency, and hatred and the ways in which they confront one another.

In recent years some social psychologists working on group conflict relations have written around the idea of "necessary but impossible" relations, sensing the weight of this disavowal and psychic disclosure yet missing the temporal aspect of necessary dependence and its simultaneous rejection, that is, the temporal dimension of impossible desire. Kelman, for example, describes a negative interdependence, a negative reciprocity based on zero-sum relations of power. Analyzing the interdependence between the Israeli and Palestinian national identities, Kelman claimed that the fate of groups such as Israeli Jews and Palestinians, Hutus and Tutsis, or Serbs, Croats, and Bosnian Muslims, groups that live in proximity, often one within the other, is intertwined, and that their needs, interests, and identities, in fact their very survival, are often defined as an either/or contestation and competition that develops a negative interdependence. Negative interdependence is illustrated by specific situations in which "each group's success in identity building depends on the other's failure in that task," or when "each group's identity becomes hostage to the identity of the other."[16] To summarize his argument, Kelman gives an example of negative interdependence worth quoting:

> In 1998, Israel celebrated the 50th anniversary of the establishment of the state. In the same year Palestinians memorialized the 50th anniversary of al naqba: the term, meaning "catastrophe" or "disaster," that Palestinians use to describe the Palestinian experience of 1948. Some Israelis saw these memorial events and writings as efforts to attack and spoil the Israeli celebration, inconsistent with the ongoing peace process. Yet even if the Palestinians were in part responding to the Israeli celebration, the fact remains that 1948 was a

disaster for the Palestinian people and that they had legitimate independent reasons for recalling and mourning these tragic events on their 50th anniversary and reminding the world of them. In principle, Israelis could have acknowledged the Palestinian tragedy and the Palestinians' reasons for commemorating it on the 50th anniversary without abandoning their own narrative or their own anniversary celebration. But insofar as the two identities remain negatively interdependent, assertion of one's own group's identity requires rejection of the other's.[17]

Notice how Jewish Israelis cannot think of the Palestinians and their needs outside of themselves. Negative interdependence is not a necessary condition or consequence of national relations. Interdependence between different ethnic or national groups in one geopolitical zone is, however, inevitable. Kelman's concept of negative interdependence mainly specifies spatial and topographical relations of identities where one identity is congealed on the expanse of the other. This frame of zero-sum game obscures the fact that under certain conditions of proximity and similarity, and particularly in intractable conflicts, the threat of dependency, its unthinkability and denial, comes to dominate the relations through the very fear of dependency.

Brewer adds yet another form of negative interdependence, depicting a situation in which love of the in-group is directly associated with feelings of hostility toward the out-group.[18] Again, it must be said, loyalty to one's own group does not necessarily require feelings of hate toward an outgroup. Yet Brewer claims that when close groups compete over resources, interests, and power, "perceived interdependence and the need for cooperative interaction make salient the absence of mutual trust."[19] That is because "shared experiences and cooperation with the outgroup threatens the basis for social identification."[20] For Brewer and Kelman the common polarized language of "us" and "them" underlies the concept of negative interdependence and characterizes a discourse of national identification. In Brewer's analysis of conflict relations, loyalty to one group is always structured around negative identification with another and the split between "us" and "them" reflects a divide between "we the good" and "they the bad." If there is a blind spot toward this linguistic divide, then how and in what ways is such a dichotomy constructed in reality?

This bipolar, zero-sum game schema of negative interdependence or ingroup favoritism and out-group antagonism is, I argue, only part of the picture. True, identification with one's own group marks the self-boundaries, difference, and distance, but what Brewer, Kelman, and others do not emphasize is the illusion, or rather the delusional element of this constructed linguistic split, the contingency of the construct "us" and "them" and the structure of dependency that forms relations bounded by proximity that are inevitable but not fixated and can evolve into murderous hatred as well as good neighborhood and friendship. These two temporal possibilities and everything that lies between them are what is at stake here.

What is an "inevitable dependency" between subjects (individuals, groups, or states)? What is the temporality of a relational space that is determined not only by necessity but also by its impossibility? The concept of inevitable dependency, or the necessity of dependency as a concept of contingency and proximity, should not be understood as a primary dependency (based on the model of child-parent relations), or as a cosmic, transcendent dependency, or as part of destiny. Inevitable dependency is a way of living socially, of recognizing the conditions of social inevitability and possibility. There are social and political conditions, mostly determined as it happens by historical events, that enforce relations of dependency between subjects, not because inevitability could not have been avoided or changed, but because those relations of dependency constitute the internal relations between the elements of the whole. In hate relations this necessity becomes an impossible ontology. Instead, hatred arises to suture the "necessary but impossible" desires that are intolerable. What is so striking and paradoxical about this suturing process is that although hatred denotes distance and detachment, in fact, and against common belief, it circumvents in present time the possibility of detachment and keeps the subject in a carefully defended and safe closeness. It bonds subjects and objects through phantasmal reconstructions, as if there were no alternative between being a victim and being a tyrant. What, then, does inevitable dependency stand for? What is the nature of its psychic and political topography and dynamics? How do inevitable dependency and hatred direct each other in practice?

All hatreds (national, racial, ethnic, religious, sexual, and so on) are based on dominant relations of one group over another, and are characterized by unequal power positions similar to the Hegelian master-slave dependency that, like desire, has no horizon or bottom. The Hegelian dependency between the master and the slave, closer in nature to child-parent relations, depicts a fundamental and ontological model of dependency within relations of domination. Both the master and the slave are not only dependent on one another for their survival and existence, but their very definition of the self is contingent on their un-separated reality. Their interdependency, in fact their very intelligibility as selves, is articulated in the paradox of recognition.[21] It could be argued that the master and the slave or the parent and the child are never equally dependent on each other, that the master-slave dialectic is never symmetrical.[22] This is of course a good point. It is true that power is never equally and reciprocally shared. If we, however, consider the need for recognition not in terms of less or more, but as a basic constitutive relational force, we can speak of inevitable dependency as part of the struggle for recognition, which indicates that both parties are not separate identities. Butler, for example, describes a radical dependency, a desire for and attachment to the other, a subject position without which we, as subjects, cannot be.[23] This Hegelian-Lacanian view of being a subject, this inevitable dependency—"For if I am confounded by you, then you are already of me, and I am nowhere without you"[24]—draws the fundamental vulnerability of subjects within the bond of (power) relations. Another way of looking at this vulnerability is through necessary relations that are not primary attachments and affiliations, but are the result of specific historical conditions of proximity which define their inevitability by the very fact of their proximity. It is not an interior structure (although it certainly can become one), but rather the comprehension of a relational (explicit and implicit) reality that is already there. What happens when inevitable dependency (as a subject position) is denied? Which discursive ruses veil (yet attest to) the anxiety of proximity?

Consider, for example, the relations between blacks and whites in America. I suppose that inevitable dependency, the very conditions of existence as one nation, but which has been misrecognized by whites, shaped, in part, the course of segregation in the United States as a counteraction to proximity. That counteraction, in turn, produced attractions and fears, loves and hates, pleasures and denied desires and needs. James Baldwin chose the metaphor of a wedding to describe the relations between blacks and whites in America, characterizing those relations through the anguish and terror of love. These ambivalent attachments, constituted by the anguish and terror of love, as Baldwin puts it, are precisely the kind of contradictions or blind spots that can produce prejudice and further eruptions of violence. Or consider the hostile relations between "immigrant" workers and blue-collar working-class citizens in America or in Europe. William Connolly writes on this point as follows: "There is thus reason in the hostility many marginal workers feel toward the alien; he both poses a threat to them and symbolizes starkly a condition they experience darkly and imperfectly. The drive of the marginal worker/citizen to maintain psychological distance from the alien contains *the fear that the actual condition of the one group is too close for comfort to the possible status of the other*" (italics mine).[25] Two points deserve mention here. First, an inevitable dependency between two groups of workers has been constituted by their social and economic class conditioning; as part of class politics, the question "Who are we similar to?" tacitly reverberates and arouses fear. The question "Who do we want to be?" becomes entangled with the fear of being too similar to those whom one wishes to separate from. Second, a related point, separation becomes a signifier of control and status precisely because of its symbolic impossibility. This example shows how fears of dependency and closeness, which are built into the social and economic system of global capitalism, are translated into class hostility and how conditions of proximity and resemblance produce antagonistic emotional positions and identities when they are feared and unconsciously rejected.

Or consider the relations between the Turks and Armenians. The Armenians of Eastern Anatolia were known as the most loyal Millet in the Ottoman Empire and a group of remarkable artisans and traders. Naimark notes that when the Young Turks seized power, they "even armed the Armenians so that they could participate in the struggle against the Islamic conservatives for a New Ottoman constitution."[26] All the same, Naimark adds, the Young Turks were far from interested in granting autonomy and independence to the Armenian vilayets.[27] There are many explanations for the massacres of 1896 and 1909 and the 1915 genocide. Most of them focus on the nationalistic drives of each side. Although nationalism was certainly the main discourse of hostility, we must not overlook the place and role of dependency, which constituted narratives of (imagined) loyalty and betrayal as part of the Turkish and Armenian reality. It may be impossible to prove, but I strongly suspect that the extreme violence against the Armenians was not entirely divorced from the fact that they were "the most loyal" group (and therefore the most loved and trusted) and thus also became "the most treacherous" and hated, in the eyes of the Turks, at the moment they began voicing demands for autonomy. Think of the loaded meaning of "loyalty" as a reverie of attachment and dependency, how unadmittedly fearful and insecure the Turks must have felt when faced with necessary dependency on ethnic minorities, such as the Armenians or the Greeks, not only in order to sustain their rule and the power of the empire but also to create a united modern Turkey under the umbrella of Turkish identity. Even today, generations after the genocide, Turks refuse to recognize their responsibility.

The above eclectic cases suggest, generally speaking, the possible direction of effects in relation to unrecognized attachment, which "conceals the possibility it denies." Now, when I say unrecognized attachment, I am saying, of course, that dependency has already been recognized and denied prior to its misrecognition. History provides many such examples. But the point is clear: Power relations produce not only ruptures of difference and exclusion but also shattered spaces "contaminated" by fears and emotional resistance in response to (conscious and unconscious) knowledge of resemblances, attachments, and forms of dependency that require the subjects to manage a system of intimacy that they perceive for historical reasons as abjection. As Sullivan acknowledges, "it is important to recognize how colonial oppression sometimes operates through enforced sameness rather than imposed difference."[28] Although I do speak here on imposed difference, as a mechanism of defense, the quote alludes to the power of sameness played by oppression. In the age of nationalized and ethnicized identities, such dependencies of shared resemblance tacitly contradict the rhetoric and politics of difference and are likely to spawn manifested actions of control and separation. This working of misrecognized dependency easily turns into hatred as the ruse of the unconscious and its invisible operation to preserve desire and foreclose *communitas*. In my emphasis on the place of similarities and resemblances (in contrast to difference) in social relations of conflict and hatred, I do not advocate going back to a classical schema of relations based on kinship[29] or to an anthropological universalism—all men are the same and so on. I argue that Western philosophy and psychology are based on discrimination, selection, comparison, and difference, which has split apart a language of similitude in order to create order (albeit illusory) and fixed boundaries. The language of difference is based on divisions of identities, giving rise not only to a new scientific knowledge but also to new social and political forms of sovereignty and justification for rezoning national territorialism and racial discriminations that resist attraction, resemblance, or historical analogies. Similarities can be overlooked, looked awry, buried, and avoided. They can disappear from language, but cannot be erased from existence. Differences are never mirrored as pure difference; the child who views himself in the mirror laughs at the other who is himself. And the recognition of the other always entails beyond any solution the paradox of difference and similarity, dependence and autonomy, love and hate.

Hate in Love / Love in Hate

Georges Simenon's story *Lettre a Mon Juge* is about hatred, but it is narrated as a story of (obsessive) love. In a private letter, Charrel (Simenon's protagonist) tells the judge how and why he came to strangle to death his beloved Martine Engelbert, in order to be happy. Charrel confesses that he was tortured by the promiscuous, free, and independent image that he formed of Martine in spite of her submission to him. It was too painful to love Martine, fearing her possible independence and incompliance. In the story, Simenon evokes the kind of love that is hate. Clearly, he understands the obsession of love, its transgressive movements, pleasures, and terror; the need to control and master she who is uncontrollable. Charrel realizes his dependency when Martine's submission is not enough to satisfy him. Simenon's study of love and hate is a drama of possession which ends in Martine's death and with Charrel's ultimate victory and coming to peace with himself.

Simenon's text on "hate in love" depicts domination as a masculine model of dependency. Here is what Freud said about the similitude and exchangeability between what he, after World War I, came to term the oppositions of love and hate:

> The other conflict, that between love and hatred strikes us more strangely. We know that incipient love is often perceived as hatred, and that love, if it is denied satisfaction, may easily be partly converted into hatred, as poets tell us

that in the more tempestuous stages of love the two opposed feelings may subsist side by side for a while as though in rivalry with each other. But the *chronic* co-existence of love and hatred, both directed towards the same person and both of the highest degree of intensity cannot fail to astonish us. We should have expected that the passionate love would long ago have conquered the hatred or been devoured by it. And in fact such a protracted survival of two opposites is only possible under peculiar psychological conditions and with the co-operation of the state of affairs in the unconscious. The love has not succeeded in extinguishing the hatred but only in driving it down into the unconscious; and in the unconscious the hatred, safe from the danger of being destroyed by the operations of consciousness, is able to persist and even grow.[30]

Many, following Freud, have recognized that love can turn into hate and hate into love; that love and hate do not mutually exclude one another, and that love for the in-group often produces hatred of the out-group.[31] Moreover, people can hate others for the sole reason that they belong to an out-group.[32] Ahmed notes that love for an in-group based on exclusive rights produces a visceral hatred toward "others" who threaten the group's claims of purity of blood.[33] But the puzzle confronting Freud was not the swift movement from love to hate and vice versa, or the possibility of loving someone and hating the other at the same time. What puzzled Freud was the possibility of simultaneously loving and hating the *same subject* (individual or group), the possibility that love and hate can overlap each other in spite of their apparent opposition.[34] Holding onto the Cartesian separation of the instincts, Freud came to the conclusion that hate has to be repressed and disavowed for love to flourish. Yet Freud warns us that hate does not simply disappear with love; it is not destroyed, but merely displaced from one system to another, from the ego to the id, from consciousness to the unconscious, still retaining its power as a psychic force.

Following Freud's idea of the coexistence of opposites, Derrida further deconstructs the relations between love and hate, life and death, in his fascinating work *The Gift of Death*. He argues that *love* (responding to others) must be repressed and silenced if one really wants to find his or her own singularity, duty, and faith. Working through Keirkegaard's essay *Fear and Trembling* as his point of departure, Derrida deconstructs the biblical story of Isaac's sacrifice. At the center of his deconstructive reading he positions the tension between Abraham's ethical responsibility toward others (his family) and his absolute responsibility with respect to his own (national, religious) duty. Arguing that giving an account to others and giving an account to oneself are unmediated ethical responses and responsibilities, Derrida declares in the case of Abraham that "a duty of hate is implied."[35] What is Derrida leading to and what is he saying here? What does it mean to say that a duty of hate is implied? Derrida develops with this statement a new "*chronic* co-existence of love and hatred," emphasizing the fundamental conflict between responsibility to others and giving an account to oneself, which is an elementary conflict between social life and the struggle for individuality and individual identity. Can we ground conflict relations within this basic conflict over singularity and self-accounting? In Derrida's thesis, Abraham had to love Isaac in order to act as murderer. In contrast to Simenon's protagonist (acting with hate in love), Derrida describes Isaac's sacrifice as an event of *love in hate*.

In order to assume his absolute responsibility with respect to absolute duty, to put his faith in God to work, or to rest, he must also in reality remain a hateful murderer, for he consents to put to death. In both general and abstract terms, the absoluteness of duty, of responsibility, and of obligation certainly demands that one transgress ethical duty, although in betraying it one belongs to it and at the same time recognizes it. The contradiction and the paradox must be endured in the instant itself. The two duties must contradict one another; one must subordinate (incorporate, repress) the other. Abraham must assume absolute responsibility for sacrificing his son by sacrificing ethics, but in order for there to be a sacrifice, the ethical must retain all its value; the love for his son must remain intact, and the order of human duty must continue to insist on its rights.

Relating sacrifice *(Korban)*[36] to secrecy and faith, Derrida argues that it is because of his love for Isaac that Abraham takes his single and beloved son to Har Ha'moria (Mount Moria): Abraham must love his son absolutely to come to the point where he will grant him death, to commit what ethics would call hatred and murder. [37] In order to show his faith (to constitute his singularity), Abraham has to sacrifice the one who is loved even more than the self. Now the implied "duty of hate" is Abraham's only possible option, for otherwise how can he kill his own beloved son? Psychoanalytically speaking, Derrida is correct to point out that "hate wouldn't be hate if it only hated the hateful, that would be too easy."[38] It is our loved ones that we must hate, he claims, in order to wholly and fully commit ourselves to our God (duty).[39] But what duty demands our hate? On the one hand, Isaac's betrayal signifies to Derrida the horrifying effects of absolute commitment to faith; every moment of our lives, he says, we stand on Mount Moria sacrificing those whom we love (could he be referring to the sons and daughters we sacrifice in wars?). He agrees with Kierkegaard that Abraham's silence (secrecy) was a horrible act of betrayal of his son and family. On the other hand, Derrida writes: "In order for there to be a sacrifice [hate], the ethical must retain all its value; the love for his son must remain intact, and the order of human duty must continue to insist on its rights."[40]

How can we decide between these two systems of thought, between Kierkegaard and Derrida? What does it mean that in order for hate to be hate the ethical order must retain all its value? In the last chapter of *The Gift of Death*, Derrida provides an answer by posing a question. It is true that the sacrifice of Isaac is a crime that should not be forgiven. Yes, Abraham is a murderer, and so he should continue to be seen. At the same time, however, is it not true, he asks, that the spectacle of this murder is the most common event in the world? On the one hand we condemn killing, hatred, and atrocities toward others. On the other hand, the law of the market in our society "*puts to* death . . . or *allows* to die of hunger and disease tens of millions of children . . . without any moral or legal tribunal ever being considered competent to judge such sacrifice, the sacrifice of others to avoid being sacrificed oneself."[41] Millions of people are killed in wars, ethnic cleansing, and genocide, but our moral system and good conscience continue to function smoothly. And such sacrifices are not even invisible, says Derrida.

What Derrida's analysis of the sacrifice of Isaac offers is a warning, a warning against a bifurcated ethical system that limits duty, responsibility, and identity to either love or hate, that averts the eyes from the invisible and the repressed, that ignores the ancient knowledge (and the psychoanalytic as well) that love does not destroy hate and hate does not destroy love; one system (or discourse) only diverts the other into silence and secrecy. Derrida's point is that one cannot give an account to oneself by silencing one's responsibility toward others. Abraham learns that giving an account to oneself *is* taking responsibility for others. At the last moment, Abraham saves himself from himself, ritualizing violence (sacrificing the calf) in order to return to the community.[42] If he had killed Isaac, would he have been able to live? This process of subjectification shows the movement of desire from love-in-hate to hate-in-love, from the visibility of hate (and the secrecy of love) to the visibility of love (and the secrecy of hate), or from repressing love (in hate) to repressing hate (in love). This movement from sacrifice to responsibility (from hate to love) does not redeem Abraham, but it induces him to say "It concerns me"; "This is my business, my affair, my responsibility."[43]

By silencing the *love-in-hate* we create a dual system of loving—loving the self and hating the other, while failing to see, metaphorically speaking, the hand of God that can stop the sword, or failing to see the conditions of possibility. What I find so fascinating in the reading of "Isaac's sacrifice" is the understanding of how much hate and cruelty are demanded in the process of national becoming. Abraham had to hate Isaac (or *impossibly love* him, as his love had to be kept secret) in order to claim his singularity. Does Abraham's impossible love (a love that could not show itself) signify the logic of nation-building and the ideology of national sovereignty (the impossibility to love others)? It is hard to digest Derrida's interpretation of Isaac's sacrifice when translated and applied to current events. Again the Holocaust haunts the discussion. I am far from convinced that the Nazis had to love the Jews in order to murder them. But just think about the intimacy and the bonds of love and hate between Germans and German Jews in nineteenth-century Germany. Can we understand the Holocaust without these roots of attachment? Derrida opens a (psychoanalytic) window to our understanding of the horrific consequences of denial, secrecy, and (religious) loyalty to the nation and nationalism above and beyond our duty and responsibility toward and love for the other but also to the revelation that hate "can only be the sacrifice of love to love."[44]

The Hate of the Other: Theories from the Clinic

Derrida's hyperbolic critique of sacrifice—the sacrifice of the sons for the sake of the nation—when love had to be silenced (and psychoanalytically repressed or denied) through acts of violence and hatred receives ample support from clinically based theorization. The following studies show that hatred, in contrast to common belief, is a form of continuing attachment when differentiation is at work as a protective move.

Decades ago, based on Freud's early views of hatred[45] and the spirit of the times, the psychoanalyst Wilhelm Stekel[46] concluded that "hate has the relation to love that disgust has toward desire." Disgust, he continued, "is the dread of contact, desire the wish for it."[47] Stekel saw in hatred a psychic need concealed as a great desire and wish for contact. In contrast to what has become the common idea that hate projects a will to kill and destroy, Stekel argued that his clinical work had taught him that in order to preserve and defend the self's autonomy, one must hate in the place where one loves. This recognition reverberating in Derrida's *The Gift of Death* also accords, though in a different way, with contemporary psychoanalytic studies viewing hatred as a form of affiliation when all other forms of attachment and intimacy are too painful, threatening, or humiliating.[48] Gabbard, for example, says that in his analytic experience for some people "being hated and hating may be far more preferable to being ignored and abandoned."[49] In his enlightening study "Loving Hate," Bollas shows that when intimacy fails, hatred keeps the self alive and in a "safe" closeness.[50] In this way hatred becomes part of one's liven spirit and is experienced as a strengthening of the self.[51]

Bollas, the strongest critic of the view of hatred as a mode of separation and distancing, argues against the psychological and cultural understanding that hatred aims at destroying external or internal objects. On the contrary, he claims, in some cases hatred answers the very need to conserve the object, to keep holding the object when love is inconceivable. Although hate can have destructive consequences, it is, paradoxically, a desire to preserve relations in cases where contact is threatening, but nevertheless needed at the same time. Based on the early childhood experiences of adult patients, Bollas argues that hatred "allowed" his patients to remain attached to beloved objects without feeling consumed by their love. Their "fear of love" or "loving hate" was a safe way to remain connected and fulfill their need for contact, even as they *reaffirmed its failure* at the same time. All these studies circulate around a similar idea underscoring, in one way or another, the notion that separation and attachment are in tandem and at once part of the very basic politics of hatred.

In Tolstoy's *The Death of Ivan Ilyich*, the ill Ivan Ilyich gains such reassurance (of attachment in the midst of separation) when loving his family becomes too painful to bear. By contrast, hate of the healthy (including his family) gives him power, "rescues" him from loneliness and fear. Daniel

Rancour-Laferriere suggests that Ivan Ilyich does not stand in front of a mirror to *see* the (hateful) "other." He goes through the mirror into a world of joy. In that world, his family and friends are loathed and despised because they are in fact beloved. Like Abraham, Ivan Ilyich had to sacrifice his family to save himself because loving was too painful. Like Abraham who was in bond(age) to his faith, so Ivan Ilyich was to his illness. Fred Alford describes hatred as relational bond(age) as follows:

> "In the novel *Immortality*, Milan Kundera has one of his characters state that 'hate traps us by binding us too tightly to our adversary. What Kundera (or perhaps just his character) fails to understand is that this is just what is wanted, hatred serving much the same function as love, allowing us to be trapped with the other while fighting against it, allowing us to pretend what we really want is to be free, but never giving us the chance. In hatred we transform interpersonal bonds into bondage, and relationships into prison."[52]

Hatred, Alford notes, is neither simply a symptom of love nor the opposite of love, but "the simulacrum of love," that turning point where love cannot find a resolution against its own impossibility. From a psychoanalytic perspective, the politics of love and hate is a central issue of life and death, war and peace. Both love and hate are viewed as limitless, unstable, powerful contingent desires; creative, dreaded, violent, and displaced, neither opposites nor look-alikes, both hate and love are unconscious forces that include each other in their representational multiplicities. Their territories are inseparable even when they apparently form different emotional and phenomenal worlds of knowledge. From this perspective, the love/hate schema represents the topography of necessary (but impossible) dependency. Fearing similarities and dependencies, groups in power deny resemblance and dependency, fighting their very possibility by putting in place disciplinary systems of surveillance and control to impose discrimination and separation that, paradoxically, continue to evade them. What is so menacing in conditions of similarity and shared resemblances?

Resemblance and Similarity

Many today ask themselves in wonder how groups that have so much in common can come to passionately hate each other with what seems a hatred full of joy. The surprise is not that people hate each other or go to war, but that closeness and similarity "somehow" end in genocidal hatred. How, asks Michael Ignatieff, can emotions within commonality stir more violence than those aroused by pure and radical difference? Why is minor difference so threatening?[53] Similarly, the historian Niall Ferguson raises the question why there was so much hatred toward German Jews during the 1930s when "there is so much evidence of love between individuals of different ethnic origin," referring to the high rate of mixed marriages between German Jews and non-Jews.[54] Furthermore, David Deutch in a daring thesis analyzed Goebbels's speeches and Nazi propaganda pointing at their "violent intimacy." Deutch claims that the traditional causal argument that relates the destruction of German Jews to their difference is only partly the case. True, Goebbels called the Jews viruses and dehumanized them in any possible way. His speeches spread venom and hatred to justify the murder of the Jews. At the very same time, Goebbels's rhetoric, claims Deutch, insinuates closeness and similarity (when one carefully reads the speeches), a kind of unexpected assumption of similarity and "understanding of the Jews from within." Deutch raises the possibility of an insider-outsider radical relation of intimacy, underscoring the violence against the similar Other to explain the Nazi murderous obsession of the Jews. There is no contradiction, he writes, between extreme violence and intimate relation. On the contrary.[55] And Michel Viviorka, interviewing Derrida on forgiveness, asks: In the worst situations, in Africa and Kosovo, do we not speak of a barbarism of closeness, the place of crime between people who know each other?

One can, of course, give the common, oft-heard answer, namely, that fears of assimilation and contamination underlie or motivate feelings of national animosity and hostility and anxieties of differentiation (national, religious, ethnic, or sexual) turn minor differences into an "absolute" difference, that groups struggle to maintain a separate and "pure" identity as a fantasy of being whole, unique, sovereign, and powerful. That could be true if one believes, and I do not, that difference and similarity are mutually exclusive psychic categories, that difference (as modern psychology attests) is the basic and necessary mode of distinction between self and other, that differentiation, the primary process of individuation, excludes similarity, and that, in contrast to similarity, pure difference is what forms the uniqueness of identity that similarity forms a primitive mode of thinking which erases national, ethnic, or sexual singularity. If, on the other hand, we approach difference within what Derrida calls the order of the *Same* (taking language and linguistic relations as a model) or if we think about difference and similarity as modes of libidinal anxieties that play a "game" (status games, war games, love games, etc.) of mirroring (alienating, differed, transferential, or common), then perhaps the answer to why "when both [groups] are the same, must one be cast out" should not be sought in the field of identity, but rather in the field of desire, in the domain of passion that turns into a symptom—"the possible impossible"[56]—that is, the field of ideology from which Fulmer (Badiou's imagined Jew from Dariza) can assert: "The Jew is not hated because he is the Other. The Jew is hated because he is the Same."[57]

In a world of "multitude" politics and power, we cannot continue to ignore the relations between politics and that underground ideology which is the psyche. What was for years denied as irrelevant comes back in through the front door as wonder and surprise: "Why should minor difference be strange *and therefore* threatening?" Why do close relations between communities and neighbors create so much hatred? Ignatieff and Ferguson, two very different historians, ask a similar question and give a similar answer: It is because of *minor* differences that difference must be expressed with hostility and hatred, they suggest. Their answer, influenced by modern psychology and philosophy, underscores the fact that difference and differentiation must constitute the sense of self-identity, in and of itself an ideology of sorts. By contrast, we can see difference and similarity, like love and hate, as double images of self and other, as forms of desire and attachments that materialize under specific articulations as hate in love or love in hate.[58]

Through this prism, similarity and difference play an important role within psychic politics of attachment and discrimination. Note that I am not saying that difference and similarity, as forms of desire, bridge between the psyche and the political, or that similarity and difference always react to each other or depend on each other as two poles in interaction or dialogue (there is no difference without similarity and vice versa). Following Derrida, I say that both similarity and difference within political discourse are passions that "structure every dissociation" in a movement of delay or retardation.[59] The formation of difference or similarity is only a question of which was delayed first. It is true that in language there are always only (historical) differences. But, in the provenances of the passions, similarity (which is not identity, particularly in circumstances of conflict and war) must be differed (in time) in order to appear as difference against the anxiety of the Same. The Same is not the totalitarian same which means uniqueness or unity, but that Same which is the background of difference and which continues to shape and delegate a nervous discourse of difference and enmity. Hence, the question how minor differences can inspire so much hatred should be looked at differently: Minor differences or large are only surface appropriations, topological distances, or political narratives.[60] The Hutu and the Tutsi, the Jewish-Israelis and the Palestinians, Christians and Muslims, and so on emphasize their fundamental differences (minor or vast) as a political tool that eliminates (yet does not erase) from discourse what cannot be said, that which is differed from fulfillment within the discourse of difference which is the element of the Same. My point is that we cannot and will not be able to comprehend the drama of hatred only by interrogating difference separated from the libidinal economy of similarity, the territory of contingency and dependency. Relations of proximity (of neighbors) stand within the libidinal economy of the Same as a platform for difference. This symbolic and imaginary proximity of affiliation and strangeness constitutes a condition of kinship and strangeness, resemblance and difference, dependency and independence.[61]

What is it about dependency and proximity that is so unsettling and disturbing to power? What is it about difference and similarity that is so alarmingly tied to violence? Sovereign states are dependent on the labor of their subjects, but even more on their compliance and loyalty. Rulers, though, unlike the ruled, tend to be blind to their own dependency. Domination tends to cover up the visibility of dependency, proximity, or similarity unless we search for them and deconstruct the unintended, uncontrolled practices of power. Rulers establish their identities (and power) through discrimination, not by the resemblances (or differences that draw things together).[62] Thus, there are several ways to speak about the connections between domination and dependency. If we again take the Israeli-Palestinian conflict as a case in point, I can single out at least three such ways by reading into narratives of Jewish-Israeli writers that indirectly outline different relations between dependency and power. These relations are mirroring, invading, and passing.

MIRRORING

Portugali (arguably) claims that there are mirror-image relations between the Israelis and the Palestinians. "Being aware of that," he writes, "is, in my opinion, one of the strongest Israeli experiences." As an Israeli, he continues, "I can attest that the Palestinian identity is a central, determinant player in the Israeli personal and collective mind, and I would not be mistaken to say that the Israeli identity and Zionism play a similar role in the Palestinian personal and collective mind."[63] Leveling the situation of the Palestinians with that of Jewish Israelis, Portugali believes that the Israeli identity as constructed by Zionism and the Palestinian identity as constructed by the Palestinian independence movement have coproduced each other, regardless or in spite of the rebuttals by both Israelis and Palestinians. In his analysis, relations of proximity, shared (yet different) history, and shared (yet disputed) territory connect between these two peoples in ways that until now they both *equally* have misrecognized and preferred to overlook. Portugali himself overlooks the fact that Palestinian history and Jewish history, although connected, are not shared; that Israeli domination dictates the silencing and exclusion of the Palestinian people and their history from the Zionist story of the settlement of Eretz Israel (the land of Israel). The equality or mirroring that Portugali creates in his comparison between the two national movements ignores the history of power inequality between these two peoples. In fact, the idea of mirroring as Portugali depicts here, is itself a form of invisible power politics of disavowal that dominant groups often generously but dangerously hold. This misconceived idea of equal mirroring becomes clearer in relation to violence, when violence practiced by two unequal groups is equated. The idea of equal mirroring testifies to the inability to recognize both difference and similarity at once within power relations, the failure of holding difference within the Same not as identity but as an anxiety. Note that, in contrast, the Lacanian mirror stage as a political reference, already conceives the Other within the order of the Same in the moment of subjectivation.

INVADING / THE MACHINERY OF POWER

Azoulay and Ophir define the Israeli-Jewish identity as a settler identity, focusing specifically on the contingency between that identity (particularly after 1967) and the machinery of occupation.[64] They argue against the mirror-image model of the oppressed and the oppressor (such as that which Portugali's personal quote reflects) and instead underscore the dependency of colonizers on their means of control and strategies of surveillance. Whether directly engaged in the Occupation (as soldiers or citizens working for the military and government), passively participating in it (as taxpayers), or as citizens who vote in democratic elections for governments that over the years have only added to the apparatus of the Occupation, Israelis are constituted as subjects by the condition of the Occupation. Moreover, Azoulay and Ophir argue that the very denial of citizenship to the Palestinian people in the Occupied Territories constitutes the terms of Israeli identity; the depth and range of the Palestinians' oppression is the measure of the citizenship guaranteed to and taken for granted by Israelis. Denying the right of citizenship to the Palestinians in the Occupied Territories is what shapes Israeli citizenship. One can overlook, forget, deny, mask, or distance oneself from the Occupation in daily life (in some places in Israel, like Tel Aviv, one can certainly do so), but one cannot escape supporting it (even when one is opposed to it) or being a part of it. Azoulay and Ophir add an important dimension to our understanding of "inevitable dependency" (a term they do not use), enlarging the scope of possibilities by stressing the direct yet hidden dependency between Israel's use of power, violence, and control in the Occupied Territories and what Jewish-Israelis have become or want to be. For Azoulay and Ophir the Israelis and the Palestinians are both subjects of the occupation, their dependency is forced and external rather than existential and inevitable.

PASSING / LONGING FOR THE ABSENT LAND

Benvenisti (a controversial historian of the Jewish-Palestinian conflict) mourning the erasure of the pre-state Palestinian landscape of his childhood, writes (as cited in Piterberg): "Suddenly I saw before my eyes the geography of my childhood, and I had the feeling that the men talking to me [Palestinian men] were my brothers—a feeling of sharing, of affinity. I could not share their sense of loss, but I could and did share deep nostalgia mixed with pain for the lost landscape and a nagging feeling of pain, for my triumph had been their catastrophe."[65] Benvenisti shares with the reader his pain and longing for the erased landscape as if he were one of the Palestinians and could still pass as one of them. But his words remain empty and hollow, a "hole," an emptiness constructed by the destruction and erasure of the past. As opposed to the old Palestinian man who is stricken with sorrow (not nostalgia) when he returns to visit his absent, nonexistent home after 1967, Benvenisti cannot (as he readily admits) share this sense of loss. His romantic pain only heightens the arrogance of his longing.

A few pages later, Piterberg cites another notable Israeli writer of the 1948 generation, S. Yizhar, who like Benvenisti and Portugali positions himself as an equal to the Palestinians. Like the Palestinians, he knows the true agony of the land; like them, he belongs to it. Yizhar (cited in Piterberg) writes: "Only one who knows to listen to the unforgetting silence of this agonizing land, this land 'from which we begin and to which we return'—Jews and Arabs alike—only that person is worthy of calling it homeland."[66] A homeland! This cruel and demanding word circles the pain and desire that tie Israelis and Palestinians to history and geography, to a place that belongs, in the minds of Benvenisti and Yizhar, equally to both peoples. Through their undivided love for the absent land, Benvenisti and Yizhar bind themselves to the Palestinians; through their love for the scenery of the land, they tie themselves to the people of the land, both Jews and Palestinians. Although their nostalgia is for the beauty and simplicity of the primeval ancient landscape and not necessarily for its people, Benvenisti and Yizhar are unique voices among the majority of Israelis, whose love of the land produces only a rivalry with and hatred of the Palestinians. Still Benvenisti and Yizhar who try to pass as Palestinians, speak from the place of domination and privilege; they can long for scenery that once was and disappeared from the land they now own. When they speak of similarity, the mirror reflects their own longing and nostalgia. From the very start (with few exceptions), Zionism failed to see the face of the other, that is the necessity of dependent relations between Jews and Palestinians out of shared destiny, and enforced relations of separation and control to disavow the anxiety of proximity.

An alternative way of thinking about dependency is offered by Edward Said, speaking in an interview to the Israeli reporter Ari Shavit. Said puts it this way: "When you come to think of it, when you see the Jews and the Palestinians not separately but as part of the same symphony, it is awesome. It is so rich and, at the same time, so tragic, almost desperate. You have here a history of polarities, of contradiction in the Hegelian sense."[67] Said, in contrast to Portugali, Benvenisti, or Yizhar, draws the similarities between Jews and Palestinians not by comparing histories, but rather from his imagination. Against the tragic circumstances of history, all one needs to imagine is the possibility of Jews and Palestinians performing together the same symphony.

We can think about language as an analogy. Foucault writes:

> For a common noun to be possible, there had to be an immediate resemblance between things that permitted the signifying elements to move along the representation, to slide across the surface of them, to cling to their similarities and, thus, finally, to form collective designations. But in order to outline this rhetorical space in which nouns gradually took on their general value, there was no need to determine the status of that resemblance, or whether it was founded upon truth; it was sufficient for it to strike the imagination with sufficient force.[68]

Regardless of the differences and contradictions, Said urges—in fact, he seduces us—to imagine the richness of interdependence between Israelis and Palestinians, the kind of cultural potency that such interdependence might promise if the players can only cling to their similarities and form a collective designation. Said constitutes in words an imaginable space of resemblance (being part of the same symphony within difference) guaranteed by the force of the imagination, not by the measure of truth. Yet, for most Jewish Israelis, embracing any such resemblance, namely, seeing themselves as part of a larger (Middle Eastern) symphony that requires mutual coordination and proximity, is yet unthinkable.

Sara Ahmed draws a direct connection between the ambivalent economy of hatred and the politics of disavowed proximity between powerful and powerless groups in colonial societies, arguing that power and proximity generate continuing implicit and explicit tensions concerning the presence of others.[69] It is the phantasmal presence of the other (more than the actual physical proximity) that creates anxiety for dominant groups who fear inclusion of "strangers." Like Benvenisti, Israelis address a narcissistic longing for the "original" "empty" land, with a "hole" that symbolizes their failure, and with hatred toward those who signify their failure. In such cases, the greater the anxiety of intimacy, the stronger is the need for separation from the other, whose very being marks the limits of sovereignty.[70]

It should be noted that neither separation nor proximity in itself constitutes the "roots" of hatred. Both are physical and psychical measures of distance in relations and have nothing to do "originally" with hatred per se until they do. Proximity and separation become connected to hatred when signifiers of dependency (love, responsibility, accountability, attachment, help, or empathy) are discursively resisted by hate speech, by legal laws of separation and discrimination, or when dependency is counteracted by mental and physical walls of segregation. But as Simenon's protagonist Charell knows all too well, destroying the object of desire (by word or gun) is a way (albeit perverse) to conserve the other as part of the self. Similarly, but in a different way, Abraham's last-minute change of heart is a sign of recognition that to sacrifice the other is indeed to sacrifice oneself.

Certainly, when dependent relations are recognized and mutual, they can in fact be pleasing, even joyous and productive. Dependency is part of connectedness and solidarity and a necessary form of sociality. By the same token, though, dependency can produce tension, conflict, and hate. The difference between these two states of effects is related not to the structure of dependency per se, but to its social meaning and cultural discourse. In a culture where dependency is theorized and perceived as an inferior and infantile desire, it is not surprising that dependency creates anxiety and conflicts in and as politics. In contested relations of desire (whose homeland is it?), dependency, I argue, becomes the nodal point of the conflict itself. The paradox is that as conflict escalates and becomes more and more violent, dependency deepens and becomes more ambivalent and distorted. The more Israel persists on separating itself from the Palestinians through administrative, juridical, or direct and indirect military control, the more it becomes dependent on its means of control and on Palestinian compliance and loyalty.[71] The harder Israel pushes for separation, the more deeply its disavowal of dependency takes hold. The "absence" of love is manifesting itself through an inversion; hatred takes over as a fantasy of power and is acted out in spaces of necessary and refused dependency.

Consider the sentence cited in Butler: "I couldn't possibly love such a person."[72] In the context of the Israeli-Palestinian conflict, the similar utterance "I couldn't possibly love an Arab" is what it is, a statement of hate but also an erased (but not lost) possibility of love that in spite of the syntax has been imagined and refused. "I couldn't possibly love such a person" forecloses the proximity of the other who cannot *possibly* be loved. It demonstrates how proximity and dependency operate in the field of desire and language, constituting the other through the topology of love and death. Similarly, in persistent conflicts an utterance such as "I hate you so much, I want you dead" can also be read inversely as "I need you so much, I cannot bear feeling it."[73] These thoughts behind the thoughts may characterize not only the mind of an abusive husband but also a specific mode of social relations with political ramifications, such as the use of harsher and harsher measures of surveillance and military violence.

Can we say that today's conflicts and wars between communities in cities, in neighborhoods, or in territories without fixed borders are "wars of proximity and identification"? It is true that wars are most often declared over land, water, and domination. Yet can we say that behind these demands lies a question of identification, "Who do we want to be or become?" and that this question is tied to another question, "Who are our neighbors, to whom are we similar?" Sovereign states and groups are usually motivated to construct a humane face and a just image for themselves. To be accepted by the international community, they must be likable and worthy of love. The Hegelian master must receive his slave's love, not only his recognition. The master, cruel as he may be, still wishes to be loved. He must know that he "owns," so to speak, the desire of the other; he needs the slave's compliance, must know himself as good. As I showed in Chapter 3, when that love is not granted, when what the master sees in the eyes of the other is resentment, feeling loved and just has to be defended. For lack of a better means of self-justification, hatred helps the subject maintain its self-image of goodness by turning the other into an object of blame that deserves hatred.

Consider those European countries that have developed a violent rhetoric ("we are being robbed of our lifestyle") and aggressive policies toward their new "immigrant" citizens (and noncitizens) from Africa, Asia, or the Middle East, while at the same time they continue to view themselves, through the compliance of these groups, as liberal, democratic nations. Or consider the many Israelis who believe that Israel's control of the Occupied Territories is just and enlightened (known by the oxymoronic phrase "enlightened occupation"), regardless of how brutal and humiliating Israel's means of control are. Prior to 1987, the ideology of the "enlightened" ruler was partly nurtured by Palestinian compliance and by disciplinary methods that were geared to raising the standard of living and life expectancy of the Palestinian inhabitants.[74] After the First Intifada (the Palestinian resistance), Israel's positive self-perception was sustained by a reverse identification, blaming the Palestinians for the situation ("Look at what you have brought upon yourselves; you deserve this harsh treatment"). In this way, both cruelty and dependency are removed from sight.

Inclusion/Exclusion

Hatred moves simultaneously between two economies of identification—inclusion and exclusion.[75] This movement guarantees that the illusion of distance and detachment will sustain attachments when attachment is necessary but impossible. In the past, contacts between nations and cultures were slow to develop; wars between states or nations were the exception to the rule.[76] In today's global culture, bodies, goods, and information travel fast, narrowing distances and establishing dependencies.[77] As a result, different national, religious, and ethnic groups explicitly and implicitly share topographies of desire and need. Paradoxically (or not), at the very same time struggles for sovereignty and national rights are becoming more violent, and borders harder to cross. As the world has become more global, hate and violence have grown; as groups have got closer, animosity has intensified. These global paradoxes only strengthen the basic Freudian dictum that there is no detachment without attachment and no repression without incorporation. Many groups today stay connected without connecting and are in relations without relatedness. Tensions between the forces that are driving toward (economic, cultural, and territorial) inclusion and the forces that are driving toward exclusion (governmentality, militarization, politics of identity) characterize today's "in-between" transitions, where some nation-states are already losing their power, while other groups and societies are still fighting to attain their own sovereign states. These transitions interplay between movements of inclusion and exclusion that are not always known or anticipated and often eclipse each other.

Contemporary wars and national conflicts show that dominant groups tend to protect themselves from inclusion, often viewed as "contamination," by preventing the other, legally, discursively and normatively, from becoming similar to them. Particularly threatening are groups that Ahmed calls "the familiar-other," those who are territorially and emotionally "in-proximity"; they breathe the same air, drink the same water, and share similar dreams of becoming, yet carry their names as an act of annunciation and difference. European countries (France, Belgium, Austria, or Turkey) call on immigrant workers to integrate and assimilate into the dominant culture, but only under conditions of invisibility and compliance which are nothing other than marginalization and segregation by another name. The nation-state cannot imagine difference and similarity at once, or difference *in* similarity; one can be either similar or different, either subservient or an enemy. Those who attempt to imagine difference in resemblances, those who are different yet can see similarities under conditions of possibility—the labor immigrants, refugees, and ethnic or national minorities—become subjects of *de-attachment* in the modern nation-state. The victims of de-attachment are everywhere around the world. Struggles of detachment feature already the operation of hidden attachments. When proximity is experienced as infiltration, contamination, and danger, hate discourses work to reaffirm the concealment of proximity and similarity. If pressed to spell out the main factors that configure hatred, I would say that they are *dominance*, *proximity*, and *dependency*. This short list, however, would be meaningless if unaccompanied by an understanding of the workings of the unconscious and its games and ruses. In order to overcome violent relations, we must take into consideration the idea that *love in hate* is never lost and therefore can be remembered.

We can now return to my opening question: Why would Primo Levi (and my father) as well as many other Holocaust survivors refuse to hate the Nazis? Is Primo Levi revealing a Derridean truth about hatred by refusing to hate? Is he saying that one must strike a distance from hatred or, in Freudian language, repress hatred in order to become *dependent without dependency*, to be left free to mourn without forgiving the unforgivable? What Levi is telling us is that hatred only ritualizes the imprisonment of the subject within relations of desire that target the perpetrators but empty the ego (and reality) of the meaning of remembrance in respect of the victims and their names; that hatred is a defense that suspends the writing and narration of the history of trauma. Primo Levi had to sacrifice his hatred in order to write. My father, like Levi, was not silent; he told and retold us his story in different ways, almost with a "pleasure" that he refused to give away in order to remember. He was concerned with remembering and "knew" that hatred would take him away from his beloveds, would sacrifice them to the duty of hatred, focusing his desire on the perpetrators. The phantasmal idea of hatred as a separation maintains dependency and attachment as fears, imprisoning the subject in a knotted relation of revenge "whitening" (blinding) all other possible affects and memories of love and life that constitute that surplus of subjection, the democratic subject.

From Justice to Political Friendship

What is the relation of hatred to friendship? Following the logic that possible means (strategies and techniques) and possible ends (violence or peace) are not always directly connected, this chapter attempts to suture the working of hatred with the possibility of political friendship in a present tense. The chapter derives from and is built around Derrida's last question in *The Politics of Friendship*: What is the political impact and range of this specific chosen word, "friendship," among all other possible words (reconciliation or forgiveness, for example)? Let me start with the following citation: "You-my-friends-be-my-friends-and-although-you-are-not-yet-my-friends-you-are-already, since-that-is-what-I-am-calling-you."[1] This designation, which Derrida, following Levinas, defines as a messianic tautology (or teleiopoesis)—how can one call upon his or her friends to be friends if they are already friends, and if they are already friends how can they not yet be friends, and so on—is, in my view, the most significant and necessary tautology for understanding political friendship, its scope of possibilities and its potential for peace in spite of hatred, without veiling or hiding ambivalence and difficulties, that is, without any idealization. I further suggest that the above utterance could be reread as follows: You, my enemy, become my friend, and although you are not yet my friend, you are my friend already since that is what I am calling you. This inversion or call for friendship under the law of the other, this logic of addressing the enemy, is the focus of this chapter. And if friendship is not yet present, it is because "friendship is never present given, it belongs to the experience of expectation, promise, or engagement. . . . It moves out to this place where a responsibility opens up a future."[2]

But this chapter is also about that responsibility that opens up the present; not a messianic present and not a present to come, but an open present. Toward that end, I bring hate and friendship together hyperbolically and raise anew the questions of proximity, dependency and distance, hate and love, peace and war, as issues that form both the issues of hatred and the field of political friendship. Note that I employ the term "political friendship" (in contrast to Derrida's politics of friendship) to depict a new discourse of peace. What, then, is the relation between hatred and friendship? And why must we turn to this classical and problematic concept in order to call off (but also cool off) hatred, when there are already so many well-formed and developed ideas of reconciliation? I turn to the concept of friendship because, out of all the different solutions to end wars, friendship, I suggest, *is peace itself.* Friendship reveres peace even though it must not be seen as whole or ideal, as entirely warm or without conflicts and temporary injury. "Oh, 'my friend,' be my friend" is first and foremost an unconditional call of desire (that outrageous desire which underlies love and hatred, life and death), but it is also a choice of peace, a sentence that decrees life. Once it is offered as a call (yes, one must have courage), the rest remains to the art of relations.

Yet, first, before I proceed with the concept of political friendship, let me examine the issue of justice, since justice and not friendship is the most common demand that always comes back into the arena of negotiations (and justice always requires negotiations) for reconciliation and peace. The demand for justice in cases of intractable conflict is understandable, but as valuable and important as justice may be, and however significant the emotional and economic importance it may have, justice is not peace, and as a

means to peace it may even hinder and defeat its possibility. I am not arguing that justice is unimportant, but only that in cases of hatred, demands for
justice often stumble upon the repressed and the denied, the desires that take
the form of an ideology of hatred. Friendship, by contrast, centers not on
justice (although it *is* an ethical system itself), but rather on relations of pleasure and peace with the other. Friendship is governed by the law of the
other (Oh, my friend, be my friend) and gives justice and equity a new social
focus and meaning. The difference between justice and friendship is the
difference between taking and giving, conditionality and unconditionality.

Most experts on peace would say that reconciliation requires an opera-
tive concept of restorative justice, such that would work through an "overlapping consensus," and in regard to which both sides would agree that
"justice has been served."[3] Rawls's idea of fair justice or "justice as fairness,"
that which most groups are able to agree upon, and which is the basis for
most liberal concepts of reconciliation, is based on "reasonable agreement"
and on the assumption that different groups can share similar values and a
desire to end the conflict, and therefore can reasonably settle for peace.[4]
According to analysts in the field of reconciliation (a broader concept than
conflict management), successful reconciliation opens a space for "security,
identity, recognition, participation and equity," issues that lie at the heart
of most conflicts.[5] In contrast to conflict resolution, they say, the advantage
of reconciliation—often an umbrella term for elements as diverse as recognition, apology, forgiveness, and compensation—is that it requires both
sides to engage in interaction, dialogue, and consensual processes, in contrast, for example, to negotiations, bargaining or arbitration.[6] Bargaining
or negotiation is much more disputative and conflicting, they say, whereas
dialogue is viewed as a more consensual and mitigated process. Many in the
field of reconciliation studies believe that "a peace that is not supported by
society as a whole will always be at risk of breaking down."[7] If certain mini-
mal and specific conditions are met and justice is restored, both sides will
be able to put aside hatred, mistrust, fear, and revenge, and open up to the
possibility of "transforming relations of hostility and resentment to friendly
and harmonious ones."[8] Note that friendship is used here as an adjective
rather than a noun, a signified rather than a sign and signifier.

However, precisely because the sense of justice—after all, we are talking
about a sense of justice rather than justice per se—requires a consensual

basis, one cannot avoid negotiations (otherwise what would justice be?), bargaining (whether dialogical or confrontational), and judgment or calculations (psychological, material, or geopolitical), dangerously repeating the conflict and driving the relations to the verge of a new potential abyss. For justice to be justice, one would need to take into account not only straight-forward claims but also national passions that have no clear horizon or visibility in language, including, for example, nonliberal beliefs. Take, for example, religious nationalism based on beliefs of redemption: Would such beliefs have any concern with a liberal discourse of rights, freedom, or fairness? Does God care for democratic justice? Note that I am not arguing that religion and democracy negate each other, but only saying that these two fields of reason do not necessarily care to contain each other. If the stability of peace is based on necessary consensus, then the act of reconciliation a priori must by definition already exclude those who do not fit or disturb the consensus of which justice purports to form a part.

To take this argument a step further, think of the hypothetical possibility of two communities—respectively, religious and secular in lifestyle—in a bitter fight over the freedom of movement (whether to use or forbid private and public transportation) during religious holidays. Such a dispute concerns not only individual anger and hurt or a history of hatred between the groups but also the fundamental question of relations between religion and state. How can these two groups be reconciled? One follows the law of God, the other the law of the state. The two communities have very different concepts of justice. If such a case were to come before the Supreme Court, as it actually did in Israel, the concept of justice would have to be negotiated and thereby become the bone of contention. What would be justice in that case? How would feelings, beliefs, and rights be negotiated?

It is clear that this kind of struggle, like many other more or less serious social and national conflicts, is not only a legal issue; when such disputes are negotiated legally (because that is the only way in which justice can be justice), the negotiations and decisions only touch the surface layer, hiding a deeper, invisible dispute and conflict about which state law has no clue. It is also obvious that any ruling will enforce measured and unmeasured violence on each side in different ways. Although this is only a minor example, it is not difficult to see that conciliating two different forms of reason and desire is not always a question of doing justice (to whom and by whom?), but must involve a different form of understanding, perhaps some form of giving or "exchange [that] does not necessarily entail reciprocity" or justice.[9] True, practice requires some negotiations, but negotiations based on fear and hatred remain negotiations without giving and recognition. At best, a resolution under the rule of law can temporarily stop the fighting. And, in fact, the Israeli Supreme Court solution (in the case I brought above) was not a resolution, but just a way to buy time until the next conflict.[10]

Moreover, before whom do we reclaim justice? Who is a partner to our claims? Do Israelis negotiate reconciliation with Fatah only, or also with Hamas? These questions are often asked and reveal a political calculation and a form of instrumental reason that lies under the surface of claims for justice. History has shown time and again that reconciliation between conflicting groups who have different schemas of justice (God's words vs. liberal rhetoric) is doomed to repeated cycles of legal, political, and psychological negotiations and bargaining, because two groups do not necessarily share the same language of rights (natural vs. political) or ascribe similar meaning to and have similar representations of peace. Reconciliation is hence strongly embedded in national ideology and can never exceed or answer the demands of ideological desire. I doubt that reconciliation as an idea of peace—which is mostly directed at reason and mainly appeals to diplomacy, political figures, and international relations—is about necessary and impossible psychic desires and about uncovering signifiers of prohibited fantasies, images, and the unthought (sanctioned not only by the norm but also by the laws of the state) such as love, dependency, or attachment. In national ideology, love for the enemy is as equally unthinkable as sexual taboos and arouses similar defenses.

To put an end to the fighting is critical, and calling off the shooting and bombing, of course, must be the first action of calling the enemy friend. It is only when the killing stops that the gesture and discourse of friendship have meaning. Once the killing is stopped, political friendship, in contrast to reconciliation, further disrupts nationalism and national ideology; it changes categories of identity and collective boundaries; friendship gives the other a concrete and imaginary place. In reconciliation, justice takes the place of love, calculations the place of uncontingent giving, reason the place of pleasure. Political friendship does not contradict justice and justice is not unimportant to friendship. But friendship is not contingent on justice and

justice is not beyond friendship, as Aristotle argued.[11] We find in friendships unequal power relations, tensions and conflicts in which questions of
fairness and ethics come to play a role, and enemy and friend are not dis-
sociated. But in friendship, hatred is sustained; it neither disappears nor appears to dominate the richness of relations, their ups and downs. Against
an economy of profit and loss, friendship is declared and constituted on the
grounds of giving.[12]

Now, I wish, for another moment, to reconsider along with justice the
issue of forgiveness, which is another oft-discussed form of giving and
reconciliation. In the current geopolitical rituals of forgiveness, endorsed
mainly, but not only, by religious leaders, forgiveness is supposed to heal
past wounds, give victims of atrocities a voice, and allow the nation to mourn
beyond claims for justice. It was primarily endorsed by Desmond Tutu in
order to prevent bloodshed between victims and perpetrators (whites and
blacks) in South Africa, and in order to stimulate social normalization.
God's forgiveness—the founding model of modern forgiveness, as well as
the basis for Tutu's idea of political forgiveness—emanates from mercy and
love; it is given to the people as a gift, not because but in spite of their
earthly sins and moral transgressions. Yet the concept of forgiveness has
drawn more criticism and skepticism than the concept of justice, or other
concepts associated with reconciliation such as equality, recognition, apology, empathy, and so on. The attitudes toward the concept and practice of
forgiveness range from strong support (like that of Archbishop Tutu, who
said that South Africa has no future without forgiveness), to protests against
the politicization of forgiveness, to claims such as that there is no past or
identity with forgiveness.[13]

Derrida's response to forgiveness is, perhaps, the most thoughtful and
complex among the skeptics. Derrida problematizes the concept on the
basis of its heterogeneity and paradoxes. In his well-known essay on forgiveness, he questions the possibility of the impossible as a concept for whose
use and workings we bear responsibility. Derrida argues that forgiveness
must remain a heterogeneous concept, in contrast to political and legal par-
dons. We cannot reduce forgiveness to one meaning or another, neither to
an ideal nor to a practical resolution. We must not split forgiveness into a
concept beyond justice, history, and politics on the one hand, and a concept
of amnesty and national reconciliation on the other hand. The religious

tradition (which Derrida calls the Abrahamic tradition)[14] poses a paradox at the heart of the modern concept of forgiveness: on the one hand, God's forgiveness is unconditional, contradictory to justice, and unintelligible. On the other hand, the sinner is required to repent, to ask for forgiveness, and to change his or her evil ways. The paradox is between a pure idea and a prescriptive concept. Derrida is opposed to the confusion between forgiveness and its linguistic contingencies: excuse, regret, or amnesty. His critique is directed particularly toward those hypocritical "theaters of forgiveness" where forgiveness is performed automatically and in mimicry, as has become the fashion (symptom?) of international and global diplomacy that supports, in Derrida's harsh language, guilt rituals. Forgiveness that extends only to restoring order and to normalization is not forgiveness. What, then, is "pure" forgiveness which is not simply purism?

Derrida does not contest the need for peace and national reconciliation in situations that involve excessive violence and suffering caused by a painful, unending war (who would?). He is certainly not an idealist or purist and sees close and tight connections between theory and politics. We must all do what we can to stop war from starting and to bring wars to an end. It is precisely because of the intersection between theory and politics that Derrida resists conceptually the use of forgiveness to normalize the social order: "It *should* remain exceptional and extraordinary, in the face of the impossible: as if it interrupted the ordinary course of historical temporality," he writes.[15] Absolute forgiveness, like God's forgiveness from which transgression begins, remains and must remain in the realm of the impossible (which does not pertain to impossibility), because only the unforgivable calls for forgiveness and only the unforgivable can be forgiven.

Forgiveness forgives only the unforgivable. And "if one is prepared to forgive what appears forgivable . . . then the very idea of forgiveness would disappear."[16] Forgiveness cannot be given on condition (of repentance, recognition of guilt, transformation of the guilty, etc.), or in exchange for concrete social, national, political, or psychological aims. It has to be granted "to the guilty as guilty."[17] If forgiveness is invoked to "escape" past atrocities ("crimes against humanity"), it loses its power to forgive the unforgivable and becomes simply a therapy of reconciliation and normalization, which, no doubt, is sometimes politically necessary. What is very clear here is that Derrida's notion of forgiveness emanates from those areas of "madness" and in relation to the "logic of the unconscious."[18] Clearly also the rhetoric of forgiveness, as a ritual to end war (a "finalized" forgiveness in Derrida's language), as desirable an end as that may be, is not what Derrida has in mind when he speaks of forgiveness. At the very end of his essay on forgiveness, Derrida allows himself to dream and meditate on a concept of forgiveness "worthy of its name"; forgiveness without conditions and without sovereignty, forgiveness without power games.

As Derrida himself acknowledges, his heart is split: we must stick to a concept that is beyond the law, history, and politics, but at the same time we have to know, as legislators and politicians, how to act responsibly in cases of crimes against humanity. This double sense of forgiveness (beyond the law and in-the-law, the contingent and the uncontingent), this heterogeneous sense, the possibility of keeping these two meanings in tandem and together, of keeping the paradox alive, is what should and must inspire the law.[19] Derrida summarizes the importance of holding together the pure and the practical, saying, and it is worth citing him at length, "This [the idea of the beyond the law, the unforgivable] shows well that, despite its theoretical, speculative, purist, abstract appearance, *any reflection on an unconditional exigency is engaged in advance, and thoroughly in a concrete history.* It can induce a process of transformation—political, juridical, but in truth without limit."[20] This heterogeneity of forgiveness, our inability to understand, represents the "secret" of forgiveness. We have to keep that in mind when we use forgiveness as a technique or principle of reconciliation: one can forgive in courts without forgiveness; the other demands justice (punishment), but his heart forgives.[21] Justice and forgiveness, both of them transgressive and lacking any center of gravity, become intelligible in politics only within the violence of the law (either national or international), leaving "dark" desires unbound. It is only when "absolute" hatred interrupts peace that the question of forgiveness emerges,[22] because hatred, like madness, is the domain of desire that cannot be forgotten or managed by reason.

What would such logic mean in the case of friendship? If we are to be led by Derrida's logic, we could say that, like forgiveness, friendship needs no reason or logic but friendship itself. But can addressing friendship become the new discourse of peace? And how can I suggest such a term when friendship is connected to a long history of wars, and when so many songs of love of dead friends celebrate friendship? And why should we turn to friendship as the new peace? After all, friendship, this "pretty tired-out term," as Danielle Allen writes, is itself problematic and given to romantic idealization.[23] Both Derrida and Allen recognize the need to change the traditional meaning of friendship in order to avoid stumbling into the pitfall of mystification or the pothole of transcendental politics, yet both continue to use it as an important concept of democracy. Following in their footsteps, I also continue to use this rich, layered concept of diverse traditions and politics instead of inventing a new, clean slate empty of politics (in the Derridian sense) but also lacking imaginative relevance. I will, of course, defend this choice and the ways I use it.

If we agree that the perpetuation of hatred signifies relations of desire and attachment, we will have overcome our "tribalism" to recognize that this unconscious matrix of intimate enmity holds, though unthought and unimagined, a place of friendship toward the enemy, the place that Freud saw as the back-and-forth movement between love and hate. As revolting as it may be (the Nazis as friends?), hatred does not mark the end of love, but only the limit of conscious desiring. And if I correctly understand Jewish-German relations in the pre–World War II period, desire was perhaps the underground bond that showed its scandalous face before turning around again. If I can, I will try to convince you that friendship in times of war and conflict is never lost despite its absence and can be called into the order and economy of recognition, into the language of peace, for the very reason that people in war never lose their desire of the other when they deny their attachment (through a narrative of difference and acts of exclusion and distance) to veil dependency and attachment.[24] Over many years of conflict and hatred, the fear of peace, more than the fear of death and war, becomes the dominant drive ruling the psyche. When desire turns to friendship, as people move into the realm of friendship, fear itself changes from fear *of the other* to fear *for the other.*

Let me, then, address the question: "Is there any point in trying to rescue friendship?"[25] Allen's answer in *Talking to Strangers* is yes, and so is mine. But I would add another question. How can political friendship turn hatred into a discourse of peace? Basing her support of friendship on Aristotle, Allen claims that, if properly understood, friendship is necessary for politics; it provides a model of political freedom, a model for solving problems, reconciling between rival conflicting desires, and is the only system based on unconditional giving, without splitting agency and autonomy from sacrifice. It is the only action where equity and sacrifice go hand in hand, because "equity entails, above all else and as in friendship, a habit of attention by which citizens are attuned to the balances and imbalances in what citizens give up for each other."[26] It is a site of reciprocity (which I term dependency), self-exposure, and shared power, not in any legal way, but in cycles of giving and giving up, "preserving equal agency among all parties."[27]

What is important is that "an equitable person displays the generosity of friendship and is content to receive a smaller share although he has the law on his side."[28] Utility friendship (in contrast to friendship based on virtue and pleasure) is the closest model to citizenship founded on equity and moderation. Aristotle's concept of friendship, however, is problematic. It is basically androcentric in nature. It is known also as brotherhood and fraternity, to which Derrida devotes considerable discussion in *The Politics of Friendship* in order to present a critique of friendship and yet endorse a concept of democratic friendship. The politics of friendship (not yet the concept of political friendship) is therefore the next necessary detour in this chapter. Allen recognizes the androcentric foundation of Aristotle's concepts of politics, citizenship, and friendship. She acknowledges that the Western concept of friendship has historically been based on the notion of brotherhood, and that such a lineage is problematic (even dangerous) for a political concept of friendship.[29] She elaborates on that danger, but only indirectly, choosing rather to focus on the category of Aristotle's utility friendship, which is least grounded in family or comradeship, in order to develop her concept of democratic citizenship that she seeks to pursue for our times.

To paraphrase Allen's question, we might ask: does not brotherhood, as a political system, re-create and propagate an exclusionary and violent practice? Is it not dangerous to philosophically and politically endorse a concept of fraternity (brotherly friendship) as a discourse of peace? Should we cease using the language of friendship altogether, or perhaps only change our addressee, revise the question from "What is friendship" to "Who is a friend"? These are some of the issues that Derrida raises in *The Politics of Friendship*. Right at the start, he invites us to ask critically: "Why should the friend be like the brother?" Why does friendship belong to fraternity? And what might the politics of any such friendship be "beyond the principle of fraternity"?[30]

Fraternity is the mirror of the doubles, of proximity, resemblance, sacrifice, devotion, kinship, homophilia, and shared death. It has a long history in hegemonic national politics as a script of heroic male bonding and a pillar of the nation. Its values and virtues are self-control, honor, courage, and love, which form the basic bond between men, soldiers, and warriors.[31] Risking one's life for a friend—a friend to die for—is the trial of modern manhood, and the signifier of kinship between brothers.[32] This tribal, familial, and androcentric commitment has turned into the ideology of fraternal devotion and self-sacrifice. It is celebrated by the nation in songs, slogans, poetry, and commemorative rituals; it is disseminated through schools, the media, youth movements, and governmental institutions, and invades both the public and private space. Male heroic friendship is constructed as egalitarian, nonhierarchical, and reciprocal in order to detach it from the erotic tension of difference and from homosexual desire.[33]

In a paradoxical reversal of defense against desire, death—actual and imagined—has become the collective space where love of the friend can be declared without fear. It allows the living friend to freely declare his love, attraction, and longing for the dead friend. At the state funeral for Israel's assassinated Prime Minister Yitzhak Rabin, former President Bill Clinton's memorable, "mythological" words were "Farewell my friend." Death allows Blanchot to declare his friendship (albeit an intellectual one) toward Foucault. That friendship, writes Derrida, "could not have been declared during the lifetime of the friend. . . . It is *thanks* to death that friendship can be declared. Never before, never otherwise."[34] So could King David sing a song of love and desire to his dead friend Jonathan, Gilgamash to Enkidu, and Achilles to Patroclus; all are epic pairs united in heroic friendship.[35] In this way the desire of the other is simultaneously neutralized and valorized, denied and celebrated, idealized and split. Through death followed by an oath never to forget or be apart, the secret knowledge of desire is constituted in its absence as the law of fraternity and brotherhood. As I have written elsewhere, the act of declaring love toward the friend in public constitutes the desire that never existed, yet always was.[36]

In this androcentric script, asks Derrida, where is the sister? What is her place in this exclusive community of friends? I suppose that this question prompted Derrida to insist on the need to come up with a new way of thinking and theorizing the concept of friendship under the same name, urging us to give up fraternization, to "denaturalize" the brother and his authority and to distinguish between friendship, comradeship, and kinship as part of the politics of friendship.[37] What then would be a proper understanding of friendship? What would do justice to its name? There are three issues here that must be confronted: how to distinguish friendship from kinship and fraternity (or, who is the friend?); how to subvert hatred and enmity (or, who is the "best enemy"?); and must the oppressed always accept the gift of friendship? What does refusal mean?

The project of deconstructing fraternal friendship, that which is based on the natural law of brotherhood and kinship, the love of the same for the same, requires a new methodology of friendship; not between equal sons, not in the name of the (dead) friend or the dead father, not for the sake of the nation, but friendship that "begins where the beginning divides (itself) and differs"[38]—a friendship based on the "law of the Other," that is, the law of giving beyond comradeship, loving before being loved, being responsible for the other that is not a kin, responding to that that differs. It is a law of the Other (and not the law of courts), based on reciprocity before equality, respect before identification (with one's own group)—a certain way of coming together with those who are not "one of us." It implies giving without conditions, calling the enemy "friend." How is that possible? Who can know how to give to the enemy, asks Derrida. No one, he writes, not yet *(noc . . . nicht)*. This is Derrida's notion of the *perhaps* but also the idea of a "democracy to come"; the possibility of friendship outside the law of fraternal love (outside love as a possession), where friendship returns to the other-enemy (not the brother) and in spite of hate we call him or her my friend in respect of his or her name and singularity.

Examples of such friendship are not lacking: Every Saturday some Israeli doctors who belong to *Doctors Without Borders* leave their comfortable homes early in the morning and travel to Palestinian villages, which are disconnected from medical centers because of Israeli roadblocks, in order to give men, women, and children medical treatment, supplies, and advice. Israel (and the rest of the world) frames (and therefore allows) these acts under the rubric of humanitarian aid. But these acts are first and foremost a declaration of friendship. Recognizing the figure of the other, these doctors give a dissymetrical gift without friendship for the sake of a friendship to come. By their actions, they are changing the discourse of giving and sacrifice; their unconditional giving is a collective gift to the other that changes the discourse of love for one's group. Many such acts of (unconditional) giving to the other in times of war are signified as humanitarian operations rather than friendship, to isolate the act of giving from its heterogeneous meaning and in order to reduce and relegate giving to the private realm of individual philanthropy (by persons or organizations), generosity and humanism. Take, for example, the case of the boy Ahmed Khatib, who was killed by Israeli soldiers while playing outside his home in the Jenin refugee camp. His parents decided to donate his organs to save the lives of Israeli children. As a result, five Israeli children, both boys and girls, Bedouin, Druze, and Orthodox Jewish, were given a new lease on life. In the movie *The Heart of Jenin*, the boy's father says that the family decided on this donation because of their desire for peace and concern for the lives of Israeli and Palestinian children. His son's organs would be a symbol of peace, he said. Ahmed Khatib's father did not speak of friendship directly. Yet his desire to see his son live on in those children, boys and girls, his desire for the life (not death) of children in Israel and Palestine, his giving in response to need rather than kinship or nationality—all this presents a way of thinking that, if supported by the power of institutions, could promote and constitute a new discourse of friendship to come. In the media, however, the donation was romanticized as a beautiful gesture of love and an act of shared humanity; as it was portrayed, so it was forgotten. The humanitarian discourse dismissed the heterogeneity of the act, isolated its giving within a rhetoric of aid and individual generosity, and hence limited the possibility it holds forth of a new logic of peace.

These two local examples, which represent a multitude of cases in every region of war and conflict around the globe, demonstrate the heterogeneity of friendship and its hyperbolic relation with enmity and hate. Every friend is also an enemy: Although these terms cannot be separated in the manner of two oppositions, the friend and enemy are two possibilities that are the same and yet altogether different. The enemy and friend are codetermined and contingent identities: "What is said of the enemy cannot be indifferent to what is said of the friend." Still, these identities are neither simply symmetrical nor plainly oppositional. This is where Derrida rejects the Schmittian opposition between the friend and enemy as the definition of the political. Against Schmitt, who advocated a concept of the political based on a split between the enemy and friend, the private and public, and who described the political purely on juridical grounds, Derrida redefines the political on the basis of multiplicity and continuous movement between friend and enemy, jailer and savior, self and other—not as separate objects, but as subjects in the politics of friendship. This implies, as I have already argued, that hate and love cannot be separated from friendship, and that even when hated the enemy signifies a phantom of possible love. Friendship has no natural friends or enmities, only a genealogy of names and a tradition of declarations. He who is called an enemy today may be called a friend tomorrow in a swift movement between hate and love. Let us listen to Derrida in his own words again: "The two concepts (friend/enemy) consequently intersect and ceaselessly change places. They intertwine, as though they love each other, all along a spiralled hyperbole: the *declared* enemy . . . , the true enemy, is a better friend than friend. For the enemy can hate or wage war on me in the name of friendship, *for Friendships sake*, out of friendship for friendship; if in sum he respects the true name of friendship, he will respect my own name."[39]

What is Derrida actually saying (if "actually" is indeed the right word at all)? What is a political friendship that does not repudiate the history of friendship *(philia)* yet disturbs the order of kinship, the figure of the son and brother? What would be a democratic friendship? What is Derrida's working hypothesis, his platform for a lasting peace? Derrida refuses to give a straight answer. In fact, he resists giving any answer at all. *The Politics of Friendship* is first and foremost a genealogical challenge, from Aristotle to Kant, of the idea (and ideal) of friendship as the virtue of brotherhood. We have seen that Aristotle's absolute friendship is problematic. So are the models of friendship that are based on pleasure or utility.[40] Other ideas of friendship, Heideggerian or Kantian, pose questions and aporias as well. Each type of friendship presents only one possibility—ethical, useful, or pleasurable. It may be true that Aristotle never really distinguishes between the three and always finds ways "that enable one friendship to be smuggled into another,"[41] but some forms of friendship are, according to Allen, nevertheless more useful (pragmatic in the Kantian sense) than others. Useful friendship, based on interest rather than love, can be, writes Allen, a good working principle for democracy which is not based on fraternity. But must we leave out love, proximity, and dependency? Can we? I think not.

If I understand *The Politics of Friendship* correctly, Derrida does not think about friendship devoid of love. Each of us must think of friendship and our obligation to the friend. We must think about the other *always in friendship*.[42] At the same time, one cannot go beyond the logic of fraternity (or androcentric love), the law beyond the law. Therefore, one must declare friendship within the law through *distance*. This Kantian distance (not separation) is the closest Derrida comes to endorsing a concrete foundation for democratic friendship, more than any other principle of friendship that he mentions throughout his genealogy of the Western tradition of friendship, including such principles as hospitality, reciprocity, recognition, giving, and equality. Distance paradoxically guards and deconstructs *philia* as a political system.[43] Distance is constituted not by separation but by respect, because respect requires the friends "to stay at a proper distance from each other."[44] Respect promises distance and distance holds respect and responsibility together. In this way love does not have to reflect union or identification. If we know how to respond to the other with respectful distance, that in itself already constitutes a certain rupture qua interruption that protects friendship and love. It seems, after all, that although Derrida never really says so clearly, he supports Kant's belief that "friends should not make themselves too familiar with each other,"[45] and similarly he sympathizes with Nietzsche's idea of a bondless bond or Blanchot's friendship as relations without relations (which also means that friends do not need to be similar, at least not in the brotherly sense). That might have been a good way out of the androcentric structure of friendship. The problems, however, do not end there: How much distance constitutes a *proper* distance, and how can the "familiar" be *too* familiar? What are the relations between distance and dependency? Perhaps Derrida would say that for Kant respect and responsibility are in themselves principles of distance, and that measurement is foreign to his own (Derrida's) thought; that respect and responsibility require reciprocity before equality or symmetry. Both respect and responsibility, as features of friendship, are defined by Derrida as the proximity of the distant and, Critchley adds, as the "utter intimacy of distance, the absolute proximity to the one who is far off."[46] Is Derrida here suggesting a dependency without dependency? And what would that be? I will return to this question at the end.

It is still necessary to address the third question I raised at the beginning, pertaining to the response of the other. When Anwar Sadat declared in public that he was willing to visit Jerusalem, he was taking a risk that Egypt might "lose face." He sent out his call for friendship and peace without knowing whether and how Israel would respond. In that particular case, Menachem Begin returned the call by inviting Sadat to come; a year later that visit was followed by a peace treaty between Israel and Egypt.[47] Sadat acted with courage. But what if Israel had refused his offer? Enemies are not always willing to step outside their "skin," outside their fears, to abandon defenses and declare friendship as a new "engine" of desire and politics. Take Israel and the Palestinians, the Hutu and the Tutsi, the Armenians and the Turks—these are but a few names that raise questions and doubts. Someone must come out and offer friendship, and it cannot be the one who has no power to lose. In the same vein, we cannot expect an immediate reciprocity, particularly in cases of excessive suffering and damage; one must have patience. The other must be addressed without equality or reciprocity, unconditionally, and with no judgment or fear. To follow in the footsteps of Sadat, the risk must be taken in the face of refusal.[48]

But suppose we can think of political friendship in present terms. How would such a concept work? It is true that every new alternative risks bringing the brother back, a phenomenon Derrida calls "semantic vertigo." The alternative would be to wait for a new language to arrive. In this gap of time and danger, I suggest going back to visions of love and hate, to the emotions we humans know all too well as sons and brothers, daughters and sisters. What *discourse of friendship* could work as a principle of peace? When I say peace, I am not talking about a perfect peace or a real or true peace, only about a possible peace. Under what conditions of speech can friendship become a political discourse? These questions, focusing not on the politics of friendship but rather on political friendship as a discourse, open up a theoretical space away from Derrida's *messianic* epistemology and the concept of a "democracy to come."[49] Political friendship must be a concept of the here and now, a concept of relations in the present tense. Although Derrida by no means avoids political questions, his view of democratic friendship speaks of a transcendent future. Critchley would disagree with me, arguing that although Derrida's *messianic* democracy, the "to come" of democracy, is "something futuristic," its arrival is in the present. Still, I argue that the philosophical basis of Derrida's messianic notion of democracy, a democracy to come, or democratic friendship, is based on a

Levinasian theology which aspires to move beyond hatred, enmity, and prejudice and thus does not sufficiently articulate the psychic prohibitions that are always with us and always imprison the future. The question that Derrida does not ask is what the friend wants from us and what do we want of the friend in order for the friend who is not yet a friend to be a friend.

I turn now to a philosophical "presentism" which is based on Ophir's ethical notion that one must avoid harm or damage that "could have been, or can still be prevented" in the present.[50] The analysis of the present offers a new framework for rethinking political friendship with an emphasis on the "here and now" and on "what-is-there" in relations of conflict, suffering, damage, and death that could be prevented.[51] Harm and damage are part of all social regimes, even within those organizations that fight against evil of all kinds. Still, one can work to prevent harm, hurt, and suffering from overtaking the other. Even democracy is always a democracy for some and exclusion for others. For that very reason, social consciousness with its passions and commitments entails, as within emotive movements, a continuous *emovere* (progression) between violence and restraint, hate and love, enmity and friendship. The principle of preventing harm as a political philosophy does not idealize love or friendship, but it also cannot do without them. It ties together distance and proximity, self-interest with the law of the Other.[52] It is the very basic meaning of responsibility, which is never only a question of responsibility in isolation. There is always another from "which the problem of responsibility emerges."[53] The principle of preventing harm is not an abstract or general notion of responsibility. It is a very specific way of taking responsibility for addressing the other. It is not a norm or law and should not become one.[54] Preventing harm is an ethical principle against violence and should remain so in order to avoid its foreclosure. It can operate as a guideline for political friendship in much the same way that sublimation and self-control work in personal friendships.

It is important to keep in mind that hatred is never absent from political friendship (there is no friend without an enemy). In political reality, however, the difference between the disappearance and the presence of hatred is the difference between life and death.[55] In that regard, the signifiers of friendship (dependency, proximity, love, responsibility) form the kind of social relations in which the possibility of hate becomes sublimated or subverted; if we are not yet friends, we will be friends by preventing harm, and this becoming, this practice, gives meaning to the movement of the present. Friendship must start in doing, the undoing of damage done and the prevention of damage that can still be done. When the damage is stopped and the possible continuation of damage averted, this preventing demarcates a new frame of discourse, a discourse of possible friendship and possible peace in the present tense.

But why would one take the responsibility for preventing harm to the other? What is the ground for such responsibility? Where does it come from? Responsibility and responsiveness to others rise from the paradox of dependency or our very susceptibility to others.[56] Paradoxically, our very fundamental dependency on the enemy (the other), our formation as people in the field of the other, our desire of the other, subjects us to the "unfreedom" of necessity at the same time that this very bond forms the basis of our responsibility to the other. It should be noted, however, that this political dependency is not only the "source" of our responsibility but also a cause for distress, resistance, and denial. In relations of conflict and hate, dependency, as I have already discussed in Chapter 4, takes an imagined ontological turn toward simultaneous inevitability and impossibility. I have suggested that the dependency between the Hutu and the Tutsi, Israeli Jews and Palestinians, African Americans and white Americans, and so forth is grounded in the very relations of fear and anxiety. Susceptibility becomes cathected to the figure of the specific other, ipso facto through the very denial and symptomization of that dependency.

Yes, dependency can become harmful and damaging, but so can responsibility.[57] The "fact of dependency" can never guarantee an automatic responsibility to the other, as dependency always works through pleasure and fear, desire and prohibition. Therefore recognition of dependency is crucial. When nations and collectivities become indifferent to the life of others, when the need of and for love is no longer acknowledged, death takes the place of dependency. If we understand the double-bind nature of dependency—the need and the fear, the psychic symptomization of politics through unconscious dissociation and its conscious indifference—we could say that the Holocaust, ethnic cleansing, and genocide in the twentieth century were perhaps extreme cases of denied dependency in its worst, most ghostly manifestation. Recognizing our susceptibility and dependency on the figure of the Other—enemy or friend—is the only viable political ground for taking responsibility for the other, not in a paternalistic (colonial) way, but in recognition of dependency as a bond that, although it may at times provoke fear and paranoia, is nevertheless a necessary force of sociality and mutuality. The principle of "no harm" and the discourse of preventing harm and suffering may not yet be peace, but they constitute an ethical philosophy of responsibility and respect that accords dependency a place as a signifier of friendship and peace.

What makes the ethics of "no harm" so promising for political friendship? To answer that question, we must untangle and reconstruct the concept of dependency. We must come to recognize dependency's constitutive power in regard to caring and aggression, hatred and friendship. Friendship and hatred do not exclude each other in a radical way, but a regime of hatred leads to a very different reality from a regime of friendship. Friendship provides a counter-discourse to hate not because hatred (or, for that matter, jealousy or anger) is erased from friendship—it is not—but because hatred can be unknotted through speech that prevents harm and damage without sacrificing the other. By choosing friendship, the unthinkable becomes possible. By choosing to avoid the possibility of harm, the enemy and the friend come together.[58]

In cases of conflict and war, declaring friendship does not heal loss and pain, nor does it erase memories of damage; no friendship is devoid of hurt, tension, and disputes, and there are "evils that cannot be compensated," but friendship recovers the balance of power. Paradoxically, the oppressors gain power by losing power and the victims gain power by reforming the humanity of the oppressors. The victims can be said to lose power by giving up the power of refusal. That is true, but they also gain power by reclaiming a distance from the oppressors in this new relation of sovereign dependency. In a situation of unequal power between the rulers and ruled, it is the responsibility of the oppressors to speak in friendship by taking the risk that comes with gift-giving, and it is the responsibility of the victims to take the gift which they can refuse. In one of his messages to the leaders of Israel and Palestine, President Obama said: "Despite all the obstacles, all the history, all the mistrust, we have to find a way forward."[59] Beyond betraying his impatience with both sides' stubbornness, the quote reflects his frustration over the need to negotiate and renegotiate. The Israeli-Palestinian conflict is a good example of how negotiations can act as a stumbling block to peace, opening new gaps and sparking new rounds of fighting and killing. I am not saying that sitting together around the same table to rework the terms of arrangements (economic, military, and so forth) is futile or unnecessary; I am saying that friendship has to be declared and proffered unconditionally if peace is to be achieved. Peace is indeed a risk of war, but one that is well worth taking for the sake of its possible rewards. We must understand that peace is not about justice or equality, but about (political) friendship, about life, love, and hate. Friendship crosses the divide between peace and war by choosing life over death, by turning the harm done to the other into the problem of oneself.[60] Of course, those who desire land more than life, who are more afraid of peace than of war, will not seek the friend. But those who desire coexistence may have already chosen friendship. This scenario goes against the real, you might say, or it is unreal, but not if we come to know the necessity of dependency and the destructive power of its denial. In circumstances of conflict, the recognition of dependency is, to paraphrase Butler, the realization that "*I* cannot tell my full story without *you*," and in order to tell it to you I must account *you* as my friend.

It should be clear by now that hatred protects the ego from the anxiety of (a threatening) proximity and dependency. Friendship untangles the discourse of hatred at the moment that dependency emerges into consciousness and becomes recognized in effective and even laughable ways, that is, when one comes to enjoy the pleasure of the Other. As most psychoanalysts recognize, the "trick" to undoing hatred is to transfer the anxiety of desire, which coagulates into a fear of persecution and of being the victim of the other. This analytic analysis fits the case of oppressors who feel victims themselves. Many Germans felt they were victims of war after World War II, and perhaps they were if we draw no comparisons. Israelis see themselves as victims of the Palestinians, the Hutu of the Tutsi, the Serbs of the Bosnian Muslims, and so on. There is truth to this analytic theory, in that such a mechanism of self-victimization clearly operates within the oedipal organization of the nation. Nationalism is founded on what Alain Vanier calls an enigmatic desire, the enigma of the other's desire, including the fear of one's own desire of the other, which is signified by anxieties of separation and dependency.[61] In that sense, the *New York Times* can encourage its readers to rethink *what* to fear (i.e., which terrorist group) and not to question fear itself.[62] Nationalism and national identity constitute the subject as a "victim" of prejudices against others whose pleasure is out of reach. We are all captives of national identifications, whether we welcome or resist national narcissistic belonging. Nationalism has always withdrawn back to the "family" and its laws of loyalty and fears. Therefore, addressing friendship to "the enemy," to the other who is outside the tribal and the familial, already negates the fundamental commitment to the nation. For that reason alone, friendship must be defended.

Where does my confidence in friendship, as a principle of peace, come from? How can we defend friendship in circumstances of occupation, mass murder, population displacement, rape, and torture? How can one imagine "the enemy" as a friend? The very impossibility of imagining friendship in the midst of war only makes it that much more necessary. Imagining the figure of the friend constitutes a different reason of the self and disturbs the logic of enmity.[63] This is a transition in thinking, a translation and re-naming of ourselves and the other, which most leaders, I dare to say, are incapable of. As Arendt argues, it has to come from the people.

In a beautiful poem, Mahmud Darwish, the great Palestinian poet, writes about an imaginary moment: "Let's go as we are / a free woman / and a veteran friend / we shall go together in two different ways / we shall go together / and be good people."[64] It is obviously tempting to read this imaginary moment of going together in different ways, in regard to the self and the other, in the context of the Israeli-Palestinian conflict and in a context of a new art of politics.[65] It is also a Derridian moment of relations without relations, of a necessary distance to create a democratic friendship. The quality of such imagined moments does not subtract from or reduce their reality. On the contrary, these additional moments (this surplus desire) in an otherwise dominant discourse of hatred can challenge the reality of hatred and create a platform for peace. However, this vision will not come about in isolation or alone. Friendship needs a friend, namely, the power of informal institutions that develop a discourse and critique of narcissistic nationalism in order to destabilize what we are and what we have become under the laws and regime of war. My trust in friendship comes from what friendship is: a principle of social life, a way of life that chooses to prevent harm as a principle of existence. Friends recognize that we are all "Others" to each other, capable of hatred and of harming each other to death; in spite of this recognition of power, though, friends resist the demands of the ego to revenge and punish by practicing the art of life.[66] In a multicultural, multiethnic national world, imagining friendship as a working principle of preventing damage and harm to the other constitutes an ethics of civil excess, of giving without taking, or in Ahluwalia's words, a "spending without equilibrium."[67] Friendship is a politics of saying no to the annihilation of life, not as a humanistic principle, but as a practice of preventing harm even when one has the means to camouflage one's doing harm under the rhetoric of defense, security, or protecting democracy.

What, then, is the relation between friendship and the political? I am not asking here about the politics of intimacy, but rather about the proximity between the friend and enemy, relations that constitute intimacy and passion within webs of interests, ideologies, and power relations.[68] My conclusion is that we must not fear intimacy, but only its disappearance. When intimacy in the form of love and hate disappears, indifference becomes a danger to humanity. It is then that genocide takes the place of hatred as a possibility and enmity turns symptomatic and fetishistic. By contrast, addressing the enemy as a friend can transform language into closeness (even if hesitant and cautious) that opens a transitional space for peace. We must, however, be careful here not to foster a misunderstanding; the call of friendship must be the duty of the oppressors; victims of persecution only have the power to refuse, which is after all also their power to take the responsibility for a possible friendship. A transitional space, where dependency and anxiety can be psychically and socially acknowledged, is the place where hatred (which is not erased) can sustain the love of the other within the self in newly imagined forms other than hatred—political responsibility for the other, for example.

INTRODUCTION

1. In 1989 my first article (with Benny Temkin) focused on the power of hate speech. Benny Temkin and Niza Yanay, " 'I Shoot Them with Words': An Analysis of Political Hate Letters," *British Journal of Political Science* 18 (1989): 467–83.

2. Niza Yanay, "The Meaning of Hatred as Narrative: Two Versions of an Experience," *Journal of Narrative and Life History* 5 (1995): 353–68; Niza Yanay, "National Hatred, Female Subjectivity, and the Boundaries of Cultural Discourse," *Symbolic Interaction* 19 (1996): 21–36; Niza Yanay, "Understanding Collective Hatred," *Analyses of Social Issues and Public Policy* 2 (2002): 1, 53–60; Niza Yanay, "Hatred as Ambivalence," *Theory, Culture and Society* 19 (2002): 3, 71–88.

3. Yanay, "Hatred as Ambivalence."

4. See, for example, Robert Sternberg, ed., *The Psychology of Hate* (Washington, D.C.: American Psychological Association, 2005), or Robert Sternberg and Karin Sternberg, *The Nature of Hate* (Cambridge: Cambridge University Press, 2008).

5. Homi Bhabha claims that the colonial discourse is written at least twice, from the perspective of the colonizers and from that of the colonized. The colonial subject he claims must be thought in the frame of *difference*. See Homi K. Bhabha, "Editor's Introduction: Minority Maneuvers and Unsettled Negotiations," *Critical Inquiry* 23 (1997): 431–59.

6. In contrast, see Talal Asad's important work on suicide bombing, which discusses various possibilities and different ways of understanding the phenomenon without justification or blame. Talal Asad, *On Suicide Bombing* (New York: Columbia University Press, 2007). See also Judith Butler's discussion of Asad's book in *Frames of War: When Is Life Grievable?* (London: Verso, 2009).

7. Andre Glucksmann's book *Le Discours de la Haine* (2004) is perhaps the most extreme one. Andre Glucksmann, *Le Discours de la Haine*, translated into Hebrew by Avner Lahav (Jerusalem: Carmel Publication, 2008).

8. For studies and surveys on Jewish adolescents' attitudes toward Arabs in Israel, see Shlomit Levi and Louise Gutman, *Values and Attitudes of Adolescents in Israel* (Jerusalem: Institute for Social Research, 1976); Kalman Benjamini, "The Image of the Arab in the Eyes of Israeli Adolescents: What Has Changed in 15 Years," *Studies in Education* 27 (1980): 65–74; Reuven Gal and Ofra Maislees, *Study of Adolescents' Attitudes toward Military and Security Issues* (Zichron-Yakov, Israel: Institute for Military Studies, 1989); Yanay, "National Hatred, Female Subjectivity," 19, 21–36; Daniel Bar Tal and Yona Teichman, *Stereotypes and Prejudice in Conflict: Representations of Arabs in Israeli Jewish Society* (Cambridge: Cambridge University Press, 2005). It is important to note that between 1974 and 1975 Levi and Gutman conducted a survey among Jewish youth in Israel and found that 32 percent admitted to hating most or all of the Arabs. In 1988 Gal and Maislees conducted a replica of Levi and Gutman's survey among 2,000 secular and religious high school students and found an 8 percent increase in hate.

9. Bar Tal and Teichman portray in *Stereotypes and Prejudice* a distressing picture of Jewish hatred against Palestinian citizens of Israel and noncitizens in the Occupied Territories. Hard as it may be to imagine, children at the age of two already recognize the image of Arabs as the enemy.

10. For example, the works of Sammy Adwan and Dan Bar On, *Victimhood and Beyond* (Jerusalem: PRIME, 2001) and Nava Sonnenschein, *Dialogue-Challenging Identity* (Haifa: Pardes Publishing, 2008).

11. A newspaper article in the *New York Times* portrays a good example of dependency between the rulers and the ruled and the place of racist (or national and ethnic) hatred in these unequal relations of power. James Philippe, a twenty-eight-year-old Haitian who lives and works in Switzerland is quoted as saying: "The police treat me like I'm somehow not human. . . . We clean their streets and do all the work they don't want to do. . . . *We need them, but they need us* [emphasis mine]." Elaine Sciolino, "Immigration, Black Sheep and Swiss Rage," *New York Times*, 8 October 2007, sec. A, p. 7.

12. In order to demonstrate the interplay between types of national discourse (secular and religious), emotional experience (of hatred), and the construction of subjectivity, I conducted in-depth interviews with nearly fifty Jewish adolescent girls, half of them secular (found in survey research to have the lowest rates of hatred toward Arabs) and half belonging to the national religious movement (found in survey research to have the highest rates of hatred toward Arabs). My analysis shows that discursive versions of reality—religious and secular—produce specific modes of subjectivity that vary in their tolerance of ambivalence and risk. I further elaborate on the meaning of national hatred as a mode of knowledge produced within a particular cultural discourse. My analysis advances the distinction between multivocal and univocal discourses, demonstrating that national hatred is not a unitary or coherent emotional

practice. Moreover, national hatred is not inherent in character but rather socially constructed through a range of univocal and multivocal discourses, which constitute conflicting versions of social reality. Yanay, "National Hatred, Female Subjectivity, "

13. Félix Guattari, "Freudo-Marxism," *Semiotext(e), Anti-Oedipus* (1977): 73–75.

14. Here I borrow from Deleuze and Guattari's discussion of the friend, in Gilles Deleuze and Félix Guattari, *What Is Philosophy?* (New York: Columbia University Press, 1994).

15. See, for example, Philip Verwimp's article "Development Ideology, the Peasantry and Genocide: Rwanda Represented in Habyarimana's Speeches," *Journal of Genocide Research* 2 (2000): 325–61.

16. In the same vein, many scholars have pointed at the relations between enmity and intimacy. Halfin writes about intimate enemies referring to demonization of the Bolshevik opposition: Igal Halfin, *Intimate Enemies: Demonizing the Bolshevik Opposition, 1918–1928* (Pittsburgh: University of Pittsburgh Press, 2007). Benvenisti writes on the Jewish and Arab people in a shared land: Miron Benvenisti, *Intimate Enemies: Jews and Arabs in a Shared Land* (Berkeley: University of California Press, 1995). And De St. Jorre refers to the war in Biafra and Nigeria: John de St. Jorre, *The Brothers' War: Biafra and Nigeria* (Boston: Houghton Mifflin, 1972).

17. That is Andre Glucksmann's thesis in *Le Discours de la Haine.*

18. Ernesto Laclau and Chantal Mouffe, *Hegemony and Socialist Strategy: Towards a Radical Democratic Politics* (London: Verso, 1985), 111–12.

19. Giorgio Agamben notes that after 9/11 President Bush referred to himself as the commander in chief of the army. That is, he took to himself the sovereign power in emergency situations. Agamben writes: "If, as we have seen, the assumption of this title entails a direct reference to the state of exception, then Bush is attempting to produce a situation in which the emergency becomes the rule, and the very distinction between peace and war (and between foreign and civil war) becomes impossible." This new situation was also connected to the new discourse of hatred produced after 9/11which began circulating among Western democracies. Giorgio Agamben, *State of Exception* (Chicago: University of Chicago Press, 2005), 22.

20. On the changing nature of wars, see Michael Hardt and Antonio Negri, *Multitude: War and Democracy in the Age of Empire* (New York: Penguin Press, 2004), 3–95.

21. Gilles Deleuze, "Three Group Problems," in *Semiotext(e), Anti-Oedipus* 2 (1977): 3, 99–109. Félix Guattari continues this line of thought, pointing that "the primary task of a theory of desire must be to discern the possible ways in which it can invade the social field." Guattari, "Freudo-Marxism," 73–75.

22. Sara Ahmed, *The Cultural Politics of Emotions* (New York: Routledge, 2004), 51.

23. The literature relates to hatred mainly as a composite emotion that intertwines anger, disgust, frustration, humiliation, fear, revenge, and so on but also as a syndrome, typology, taxonomy, or disposition. See, for example, Sternberg, *Psychology of Hate*. I do not subscribe to any of these definitions. I do make a distinction between hatred related to humiliation (often expressed by oppressed people) and hatred related to the threat of losing power and control (often a misrecognized hatred of the sovereign).

24. Judith Butler, *The Psychic Life of Power: Theories of Subjection* (Palo Alto, Calif.: Stanford University Press, 1997).

25. Marco Belpoliti and Robert Gordon, eds., *The Voice of Memory: Interviews with Primo Levi 1961–1987* (Cambridge: Polity Press, 2001), 204.

26. Robert Sternberg proposes a theoretical typology of hate in which one of its action-feeling principles is the negation of intimacy. In contrast I claim that the aim of hatred is to preserve closeness and intimacy when both are normatively "forbidden" and impossible. Robert J. Sternberg, "Understanding and Combating Hate," in Sternberg, *The Psychology of Hate* (Washington, D.C.: American Psychological Association, 2005), 37–49.

27. Such are, for example, the activities of Doctors Without Borders or the day trips started by the Israeli activist Ilana Hamerman, in which Palestinian girls and women from the West Bank are smuggled to Tel Aviv for a day of fun, relaxation, and enjoyment by Israeli peace activists. See Holly Epstein Ojalvo, "Fun, and Risks, at the Beach in Tel Aviv," *New York Times*, 28 July 2011. learning.blogs.nytimes.com/2011/07.

28. In contrast to Agamben's "state of necessity," also conceived as a state of exception—a subjective fact that serves to justify "a single, specific case of transgression by means of an exception"—psychic necessity signifies the rule, not the exception; the objective, not the subjective. The rule of psychic necessity is a surplus within and beyond the politics of conflict. Therefore, in times of (national or civil) war, we can speak of necessity in psychic terms and of states of necessity as an exception in relation to the law as two unrelated political consequences of the ideology of hatred that might or might not coexist. For a further elaboration of the concept "state of necessity," see Agamben, *State of Exception*, 24–31.

29. Albert Memmi, *The Colonizer and the Colonized* (Boston: Beacon Press, 1965).

30. Eyal Weizman, "Thanato-Tactics," in *The Power of Inclusive Exclusion: Anatomy of Israeli Rule in the Occupied Palestinian Territories*, ed. Adi Ophir, Michal Givoni, and Sari Hanafi (New York: Zone Books, 2009), 543–73; Adi Ophir, *The Order of Evils: Toward an Ontology of Morals* (New York: Zone Books, 2005). Weizman and Ophir discuss the strategy of "lesser evil" as a

colonization politics that maintains a constant gap between possible and actual aggression not to demonstrate the benevolence of the colonizer, but as a tactic to keep the population constantly facing the threat of a possible catastrophe if they do not submit to colonial rule or if they rebel against it. This strategy also demonstrates Memmi's problematization of the colonizers' ambivalent dependency in the colonial situation: the need to keep the colonized subject alive and at the same time project the fantasy of annihilating him.

31. Jacques Lacan, *The Four Fundamental Concepts of Psycho-Analysis* (New York: W. W. Norton & Company, 1973), 203.

32. Memmi pays close attention to the ambivalent position of the *good willing occupier*, the Communist or Socialist who supports the colonized in his or her struggles against occupation and is willing to enlist in the struggle together with the colonized but receives a cold response and suspicion, to which he or she reacts in bewilderment and disappointment. Albert Memmi, *The Colonized and the Colonizer* (Boston: Beacon Press, 1965).

33. This process, however, takes place without the reflection of the subject.

34. Fred Botting and Scott Wilson, eds., *The Bataille Reader* (Oxford: Blackwell, 1997), 334.

35. Foucault reflects on Bataille's method of writing in similar terms. He claims that Bataille writes as if he has to kill God in every sentence, to lose his language "in the dead of night," as if he must cross the horizon of the uncrossable. Michel Foucault, "Preface to Transgression," in *Language, Counter-Memory, Practice*, ed. Donald F. Bouchard (Ithaca, N.Y.: Cornell University Press, 1977), 29–52.

36. During the academic year 1996–97, I moderated together with two other moderators from the School for Peace in Nave Shalom–Wahat El Salam (a Jewish-Arab village near Jerusalem) a dialogue group as part of the course on the Psychological and Social Processes in Light of the Arab-Jewish Conflict. The participants, eight Jewish and eight Arab students, met once a week for three hours throughout the academic year to discuss issues related to the conflict. The dialogue gave the students an opportunity to "bring" the conflict into the room and discuss each other's experiences, prejudices and stereotypes, fears and hopes. All the quotes in this chapter are translated from the Hebrew transcripts recorded (with the permission of the group) at every meeting throughout the year. For further information, discussion, and critique of this particular group, see Sara Helman, "Monological Results of Dialogue: Jewish-Palestinian Encounter Groups as Sites of Essentialization," *Identities: Global Studies in Culture and Power* 9 (2002): 327–54.

37. Niall Ferguson, *The War of the World: Twentieth-Century Conflict and the Descent of the West* (London: Penguin Books, 2006), 651. Ferguson writes that according to the War Project there were at least 200 interstate or civil wars between 1900 and 1990, and that according to the Stockholm International

Peace Research Institute there were over a hundred armed conflicts in the last decade.

38. In the movies *Jaffa, The Orange's Clockwork* (Alma Films, 2009) directed by Eyal Sivan and *Hotel Rwanda* (United Artists, 2004) directed by Terry George, we can hear Jews and Palestinians, Hutus and Tutsis speak about their relations prior to the war in terms of reciprocity, neighborly relations, and closeness.

39. Hardt and Negri, *Multitude.*

40. Slavoj Žižek, *Violence* (New York: Picador Press, 2008), 204.

I. HATRED AND ITS VICISSITUDES

1. Michal Hardt and Antonio Negri, *Multitude: War and Democracy in the Age of Empire* (New York: Penguin Press, 2004), 3–95.

2. Edward B. Royzman, Clark McCauley, and Paul Rozin, "From Plato to Putnam: Four Ways to Think About Hate," in *The Psychology of Hate*, ed. Robert Sternberg (Washington, D.C.: American Psychological Association, 2005), 3–35.

3. bell hooks, *Killing Rage, Ending Racism* (New York: Holt and Company, 1995), 30.

4. Helene Cixous, "Bare Feet," in *An Algerian Childhood: A Collection of Auto-biographical Narratives*, ed. Leilla Sebbar (Minneapolis, MN: Ruminator Books, 2001), 49.

5. hooks, *Killing Rage*, p. 11

6. Ibid., p. 17

7. Ibid., p. 16.

8. Wendy Brown, "Wounded Attachments," in *States of Injury: Power and Freedom in Late Modernity* (Princeton, N.J.: Princeton University Press, 1995), 52–76.

9. Ibid., 27.

10. I use the term "colonized subjects" here not to allude to the colonial period, but as a general term for subjection.

11. Walter Benjamin, "Critique of Violence," in *Selected Writings*, vol. 1 (Cambridge, Mass.: Harvard University Press, 1999), 277–300. For a different philosophical position that argues against legitimate violence (but self-defense), see Hannah Arendt, *On Violence* (New York: Harcourt, Brace and World, 1970).

12. Carl Schmitt, *The Concept of the Political* (Chicago: University of Chicago Press, 1996). In his work on the concept of the political, Schmitt argues that, like the domains of the social, economic, moral, or aesthetic, the political must have its own "ultimate" distinction "to which all action with a specifically political meaning can be traced" (p. 26). The category that he marked as the

most specific to the political field and to which political actions and motives can be reduced is the distinction between friend and enemy.

13. See Leo Strauss's notes on Schmitt's concept of the political in *The Concept of the Political*, 2nd ed. (Chicago: University of Chicago Press, 2007), particularly p. 102. Also see Wendy Brown, *Walled States, Waning Sovereignty* (New York: Zone Books, 2010).

14. Some might oppose Schmitt as an authoritative political thinker because of his Nazi affiliation. Here, however, I follow Chantal Mouffe's sentiment saying that one can "use Schmitt against Schmitt." I also agree with Mouffe that Schmitt's criticism of liberal pluralism is a good opportunity to rethink critically concepts of cosmopolitan citizenship, democratic politics, and concepts of unity including the meaning of inclusion and exclusion. Chantal Mouffe, ed., "Carl Schmitt and the Paradox of Liberal Democracy," *The Challenge of Carl Schmitt* (London: Verso, 1999), 38–53.

15. For example, Bowden notes that "yesterday's terrorists can become tomorrow's heads of state and government. . . . Examples abound from the Roman Empire, to Jacobins, to much of the postcolonial world, where revolutionaries once labeled as terrorists by the colonial powers later wrote themselves into history as freedom-fighters and liberationists. Their vanquished overlords on the other hand were in turn labeled as enemies of the people, state terrorists, tyrants, imperialists, et cetera." Brett Bowden, "The Terror(s) of Our Time(s)," *Social Identities* 13 (2007): 4, 545.

16. Judith Butler, *Bodies That Matter: On the Discursive Limits of "Sex"* (New York: Routledge, 1993), 307.

17. In *Precarious Life*, Butler writes that "'terrorism' becomes the name to describe the violence of the illegitimate, whereas legal war becomes the prerogative of those who can assume international recognition as legitimate states." This is a good example of a politics of supremacy and patronage by those who have the (military, economic, and legal) power to define which wars are legitimate and just and which are "terrorist" attacks. The word "terrorism" is also an example of the play on words that becomes discourse and policy. Judith Butler, *Precarious Life: The Power of Mourning and Violence* (London: Verso, 2004), 88.

18. Michael Slackman, "Book Sets off Immigration Debate in Germany," *New York Times*, 2 September 2010, sec. A, p. 4.

19. Giorgi Agamben, *The Open: Man and Animal* (Stanford, Cailf.: Stanford University Press, 2004), 37.

20. Ibid., 15.

21. Ibid., 16.

22. Ibid., 77.

23. Ibid., 22.

24. Ibid., 80.

25. There are works of art and poetry that use a language of abjection to transgress language, to reach a "no man's land" where the monstrous takes control over their semiotics, where words and images touch the nerves, where language works against itself, creating great beauty. Such are the writings of Bataille or Saline. Bataille writes with a passion for total fusion with the other in order to touch the horror of the orgasmic feeling of living. In his writing, erotic desire and hatred, disgust and delight, are not alien to each other. Bataille wishes to form a language that captures limit-experiences, the edge of actions that cross the lines between the inside and the outside, self and other, experiences of being and the absence of being at once. See all Foucault's comments on Bataille, "Preface to Transgression," in *Language, Counter-Memory, Practice*, ed. Donald F. Bouchard (Ithaca, N.Y.: Cornell University Press, 1977), 29–52.

26. In her book *Hatred and Forgiveness*, Kristeva emphasizes that abjection is not a passive position of seduction-invasion but "a reciprocal situation of attraction-and-repulsion." Julia Kristeva, *Hatred and Forgiveness* (New York: Columbia University Press, 2010), 160. Likewise, I see abjection as a multiplicity of contradictory forces working simultaneously.

27. For the precise quote see Sara Ahmed, *The Cultural Politics of Emotions*, (New York: Routledge, 2004), 51.

28. Victoria Wohl, *Love among the Ruins: The Erotics of Democracy in Classical Athens* (Princeton, N.J.: Princeton University Press, 2002).

29. Gilles Deleuze, "Three Group Problems," in *Semiotext(e)*, *Anti-Oedipus* 2 (1977): 3, 99–109.

2. THE POLITICAL UNCONSCIOUS

1. I was inspired and influenced by Fredric Jameson's concept of the political unconscious. Jameson suggests a postmodern concept to interpret history as the "absent cause" (the collective representation) of literary texts. He writes: "All literature, no matter how weakly, must be informed by what we have called a political unconscious, that all literature must be read as a symbolic meditation on the destiny of community." Jameson prefers to use history as the "absent cause" of a text because "history," in contrast to "desire," has *a reality* of social contradictions which can be traced back by semiotic analysis. Following Jameson, the social sciences have referenced the political unconscious to the logic of hegemonic discourses, which grant power to certain texts and marginalize and exclude others. I have taken a somewhat different path and propose to reference the concept of the political unconscious to a reality of conflict by performing a dual circular analysis, from expressions and acts of control and violence to asking ourselves what these acts "want" or "need." For further elaborations on Jameson's concept of the political unconscious, see Fredric Jameson, *The Politi-*

cal Unconscious: Narrative as a Socially Symbolic Act (Ithaca, N.Y.: Cornell University Press, 1981); Steve Seidman, *Difference Troubles: Queering Social Theory and Sexual Politics* (Cambridge: Cambridge University Press, 1997).

2. Particularly with Butler's *The Psychic Life of Power: Theories of Subjection* (Palo Alto, Calif.: Stanford University Press, 1997).

3. Sigmund Freud, "The Unconscious [1915]," in *General Psychological Theory*, ed. Philip Rieff (New York: Collier Books, 1963), 116–150.

4. Victoria Wohl claims that historical, political, and literary texts are the location of desire's articulation. Victoria Wohl, *Love among the Ruins: The Erotics of Democracy in Classical Athens* (Princeton, N.J.: Princeton University Press, 2002).

5. Freud developed the idea that psychic contents enter consciousness or the external reality as a symptom or a substitute-formation. Similarly, Wohl's comments on the "Athenian unconscious" are also particularly relevant. Wohl, *Love among the Ruins*, 28.

6. See Gilles Deleuze, "Three Group Problems," *Semiotext(e), Anti-Oedipus*, 2 (1977): 3, 99–109.

7. More specifically, I will discuss and develop Freud's ideas that psychoanalysis regards consciousness as a quality of the psyche, that psychic (unconscious) ideas have the same effects that ordinary ideas have, in spite of the fact that they do not become conscious, that certain forces prevent some ideas from becoming conscious, and that cathected thoughts, thoughts that are attached to desire, are held to be true. These claims suggest that unconscious and conscious thought work together to form the politics of desire.

8. According to Jameson, Freud "was in no position to understand the consequences of his discovery." Cited in William Dowling, *Jameson, Althusser, Marx: Introduction to the Political Unconscious* (London: Methuen, 1984), 114.

9. In relation to the incest taboo, Freud holds a Darwinian functional theory that stresses the necessity of the law for the survival of the community. In Freud's mind, it was only natural that kin relations, the place of care, love, and trust, should be the main and primary venue for fantasies of sexual desire. Sigmund Freud, *Group Psychology and the Analysis of the Ego*, trans. James Strachey (New York: W. W. Norton, 1959).

10. For a critique of the liberal reading of Freud's social psychology, see Wendy Brown "Subjects of Tolerance: Why We Are Civilized and They Are the Barbarians," in *Political Theologies: Public Religions in a Post-Secular World*, ed. Hent de Vries and Lawrence E. Sullivan (New York: Fordham University Press, 2006), 298.

11. In his lecture "The Unconscious," Freud argued that the unconscious has a greater compass and that repression is a part of the unconscious, p. 116.

12. See Jean Laplanche, *Essays on Otherness* (New York: Routledge, 1999). Particularly see his essay "A Short Treatise on the Unconscious," pp. 84–116.

13. Prior to language acquisition, the pre-linguistic child is dominated by pleasure and pain.

14. Here I borrow Wohl's concept in *Love among the Ruins* of democratic desire or democratic love to describe the compliance of the Athenian people with the law of the dictator and Athens in the name of the love of the dictator.

15. In Lacan's theory, a signifier "is that which represents a subject for another signifier." In this sense almost everything emerges from the structure of the signifier. The master signifier, the *point de caption*, is always primarily the phallus, the main object of desire. Jacques Lacan, *The Four Fundamental Concepts of Psycho-Analysis*, trans. Jacques-Alain Miller (New York: W. W. Norton, 1973), 206–7. Many scholars have used the concept of the "master signifier" in a more extended, interpretative way. For example, Laclau and Mouffe relate to the master signifier as that category that "involves the notion of a particular element assuming a 'universal' structuring function within a certain discursive field." Ernesto Laclau and Chantal Mouffe, *Hegemony and Socialist Strategy: Towards a Radical Democratic Politics* (London: Verso, 2001).

16. Pierre Bourdieu defined the "community of unconsciousness" as a community that "provides each of its members with the experience of an exaltation of the ego, the principle of solidarity rooted in attachment to the group as an enchanted image of the self." Pierre Bourdieu, *Sketch for a Self-Analysis* (Chicago: University of Chicago Press, 2004), 7–8.

17. See Butler, *Psychic Life*.

18. Georges Canguilhem, "Introduction to Penser la folie: Essais sur Michel Foucault," in *Foucault and His Interlocutors*, ed. Arnold I. Davidson (Chicago: University of Chicago Press, 1997), 33–35.

19. Foucault argues against the human sciences that produce knowledge (order) in order to control the "continuous descent [of man] towards death." Michel Foucault, *The Order of Things: An Archaeology of the Human Sciences* (New York: Vintage Books, 1970). Particularly see pp. 344–87.

20. A dialogue with Michel Foucault, David Coper, Jean-Pierre Faye, Marie-Odile, and Marine Zecca, in *Michel Foucault, Politics, Philosophy, Culture: Interviews and Other Writings 1977–1984*, ed. Lawrence D. Kritzman (New York: Routledge, 1988), 208.

21. Lawrence D. Kritzman, ed., *Michel Foucault, Politics, Philosophy, Culture: Interviews and Other Writings 1977–1984*, (New York: Routledge, 1988), 322.

22. Ibid., 326.

23. Ibid., 327.

24. Ibid., 325.

25. See Jacques Derrida, "To Do Justice to Freud: The History of Madness in the Age of Psychoanalysis," in *Foucault and His Interlocutors*, ed. Arnold I. Davidson (Chicago: University of Chicago Press, 1997), 57–96.

26. Foucault, "Madness, the Absence of Work," in *Foucault and His Interlocutors*, ed. Arnold I. Davidson (Chicago: University of Chicago Press, 1997), 97–104.

27. Ibid., 63.

28. Ibid., 62.

29. Foucault, *Order of Things*, 375.

30. Ibid., 375.

31. Foucault, "Madness, and the Absence of Work," in *Foucault and His Interlocutors*, ed. Arnold I. Davidson (Chicago: University of Chicago Press, 1997), 102.

32. I am relying here in particular on Foucault's article "Madness, the Absence of Work," in Davidson, *Foucault and His Interlocutor*, 97–104.

33. Foucault, *Order of Things*, 66.

34. Foucault, "Madness, the Absence of Work," in Davidson, *Foucault and His Interlocutors*, 100.

35. I have borrowed the term "cover operation" from Jean-Pierre Faye in his dialogue with Michel Foucault. Kritzman, *Michel Foucault*, 180.

36. I thank Joan Wallach Scott for pointing out the need for this clarification.

37. Žižek justifiably warns us against a commonsense notion of "primordiality." Still, there are moments, particularly when he talks about desire acquiring a spectral autonomy, that he can be read as denouncing capitalism's false consciousness draped in a sophisticated psychoanalytic cloak. Because he gives the Real (the topography of desire which resists culture and symbolization) such an essential place, his theory of ideology, the slippage of desire into representation, can easily be reduced to a traditional Marxist notion of false consciousness. Yet, I believe we should resist such reading. The "ideology of desire," a psychic yet social phenomenon, contributes to our understanding not only of art and cultural products but also of political events.

38. See Jacques Derrida, "For the Love of Lacan," in *Resistances of Psychoanalysis*, trans. Peggy Kamuf, Pascal-Anne Brault, and Michael Naas (Stanford, Calif.: Stanford University Press, 1996), 58.

39. Slavoj Žižek, "The Spectre of Ideology," in *Mapping Ideology* (London: Verso, 1994), 3.

40. Ibid., 4.

41. Ibid., 21.

42. Michael Billig addresses a similar idea in *Freudian Repression: Conversation Creating the Unconscious* (Cambridge: Cambridge University Press, 1999), 187.

43. Ibid., 23.

44. In "For the Love of Lacan," Derrida criticizes Lacan's concept of the Real, which leans on an idealized concept of truth. Lacan's truth is the truth of

the phallus as a transcendental signifier. Derrida asked: Is there an "outside-the-archive"? Is it possible to view "truth" or "desire" or the unconscious itself outside collective memory? Is there an "outside-the-society," an outside of time and space?

45. In a different way, Ralph Ellison treats his uncontrollable laughter in the play *Tobacco Road*, the dramatized theatrical version of Erskine Caldwell's novel by Jack Kirkland in 1936, as "blowing his cover," exposing his "true" southern nature, stripping the New Yorker's mask off his face. In both cases laughter is a symptom. For Žižek it is an ideological fantasy, for Ellison an extraditing "trouble."

46. Žižek himself poses the question: "Is not the symptom a symbolic formation par excellence, a cipher, a coded message which can be dissolved through interpretation because it is already in itself a signifier?" Slavoj Žižek, *The Sublime Object of Ideology* (London: Verso, 1989), 73.

47. Toward the end of *The Sublime Object of Ideology* (pp. 163–64), Žižek makes an effort to settle the paradox of the Real—that hard kernel which resists symbolization, which does not really exist, yet has concrete effects on its subject—by distinguishing methodologically between existence per se and the properties of desire. So, in reply to the question "Why forbid something which is already in itself impossible?" his answer is: because "the prohibition relates to the properties it predicates" and not to the level of its existence or nonexistence. That distinction allows me to perform the leap from the Real to desire, and to locate desire in the political unconscious in relation to the power of forbidden possibilities and prohibitions that are already part of the discursive domain.

48. Butler, *Psychic Life*, 11.

49. Butler also claims that "the purposes of power are not always the purposes of agency." *Psychic Life*, 15.

50. Ibid., 18.

51. Ibid., 19.

52. Ibid., 9.

53. Ibid., 134.

54. Ibid., 143.

55. This is how Butler puts it in her own words: "If melancholia appears at first to be a form of containment, a way of internalizing an attachment that is barred from the world, it also establishes the psychic conditions for regarding "the world" itself as contingently organized through certain kinds of foreclosures." *Psychic Life*, 143.

56. Ibid., 168.

57. Ibid., 174.

58. Ibid., 177.

59. Ibid., 120.

60. The use of idealization is already depicting the absence of the subject as a real person. In this way the speaker captures both the desire of the other and its impossibility as part of speech and identity.

61. This utterance is a takeoff on Butler's capturing "It's not true, I am not a lesbian."

62. See Charles F. Alford, "Hatred as Counterfeit Community and the Simulacrum of Love," *Journal of the Psychoanalysis of Culture & Society* 2 (1997): 1, 39–45; Christofer Bollas, "Loving Hate," *Annual Journal of Psychoanalysis* 12 (1984): 221–37; Niza Yanay, "Hatred as Ambivalence," *Theory, Culture and Society* 19 (2002): 3, 71–88.

63. Along a similar thought, Shannon Sullivan and Nancy Tuana edited a revealing collection of articles around the concept "epistemologies of ignorance." In their introduction they write: "Sometimes what we do not know is not mere gap in knowledge, the accidental result of an epistemological oversight. Epistemologically in the case of racial oppression, a lack of knowledge or an unlearning of something previously known often is actively produced for purposes of domination and exploitation"; in *Race and Epistemologies of Ignorance*, ed. Shannon Sullivan and Nancy Tuana (New York: State University of New York Press, 2007), 1.

64. Slavoj Žižek, *Violence* (New York: Picador Press, 2008), 53.

65. Žižek's phrase "the enigma of desire" is used by Wohl, *Love among the Ruins*, 223. Related to this discussion is Mills's concept of white ignorance connected to white supremacy. Sullivan and Tuana, *Race and Epistemologies*, 13–38.

66. The Israeli historian Benny Morris, who otherwise wrote some important books on the Israeli-Palestinian conflict since 1948, admitted in *Haaretz* newspaper his regret that Ben-Gurion, who ordered the expulsion of Palestinians from their homes and the destruction of more than 400 of their villages, did not finish his task and did not expel all the Arab population from the State of Israel. Such a confession signifies the fantasy of many Jewish-Israelis to erase the Palestinian "problem" from their existence.

3. THE MECHANISMS OF SOCIAL IDEALIZATION AND SPLITTING

1. For example, see Noelle McAfee, *Democracy and the Political Unconscious* (New York: Columbia University Press, 2008); Emma Hutchison and Roland Bleiker, "Emotional Reconciliation: Reconstructing Identity and Community after Trauma," *European Journal of Social Theory* 11 (2008): 3, 385–403.

2. Elisabeth Young-Bruehl, *Where Do We Fall When We Fall in Love?* (New York: Other Press, 2003); Alain Badiou, *Ethics: An Essay on the Understanding of Evil*, trans. Peter Hallward (London: Verso, 2001).

3. Slavoj Žižek, *Violence* (New York: Picador, 2008), 62.

4. See Hutchison and Bleiker, "Emotional Reconciliation," 390; Daniel Bar Tal, "Why Does Fear Override Hope in Societies Engulfed by Intractable Conflict, as It Does in the Israeli Society?" *Political Psychology* 2 (2001): 602.

5. McAfee, *Democracy and the Political Unconscious,* 49.

6. See Lynne Layton, "Cultural Hierarchies, Splitting, and the Heterosexist Unconscious" in *Bringing the Plague: Toward a Postmodern Psychoanalysis,* ed. Susan Fairfield, Lynne Layton, and Carolyn Stack (New York: Other Press, 2002), 195–223. Also, Alain Badiou, *Ethics.*

7. The group that I quote here is the same group I describe in the Introduction, footnote 36.

8. For example, Zonnenshein and Halabi describe in details their unique project of working with Jewish-Palestinian dialogue groups at the school for peace, Nave Shalom/Wahat El Salam. Nava Zonnenshein and Rabah Halabi, "Consciousness, Identity and the Challenge of Reality: The Work Approach of the School for Peace," in *Dialogue between Identities: Arabs and Jews in Nave Shalom,* ed. Rabah Halabi (Tel Aviv: Hakibbutz Hameuchad, 2000), 16–27. Hebrew.

9. This is a well-known experience of the oppressed. For example, David Roediger (in Mills's article "White Ignorance") remarks that "colored people of this country know and understand the white people better than the white people know and understand them." See Charles Mills, "White Ignorance," in *Race and Epistemologies of Ignorance,* ed. Shannon Sullivan and Nancy Tuana (New York: State University of New York Press, 2007), 17.

10. Simon Clarke, "Splitting Difference: Psychoanalysis, Hatred and Exclusion," *Journal for the Theory of Social Behaviour* 29 (1999): 30.

11. Sara Ahmed, *Strange Encounters: Embodied Others in Post-Coloniality* (New York: Routledge, 2000), 97.

12. Frank M. Lachmann and Robert Stolorow, "Idealization and Grandiosity: Developmental Considerations and Treatment Applications," *Psychoanalytic Quarterly* 45 (1976): 566.

13. The idealization of Palestinians in the context of Jewish-Palestinian dialogue groups has also been noted by other studies. For example, see Rabah Halabi and Nava Zonnenshein. "The Jewish-Palestinian Encounter in Time of Crisis," *Journal of Social Issues* 60 (2004): 2, 373–89; Nadim N. Rouhana, *Palestinian Citizens in an Ethnic Jewish State: Identities in Conflict* (New Haven, Conn.: Yale University Press, 1997).

14. Freud, S, "The Unconscious," in *General Psychological Theory* (New York: Collier Books, 1963), 108.

15. In contrast to the Lacanian notion of split subject, I focus here on Klein's notion of the splitting of the object. As I will show later, Klein's concept is salient to the view of splitting as a mechanism of discourse. For an interest-

ing and convincing thesis on Klein as a social theorist, see Fred Alford, *Melanie Klein and Critical Social Theory: An Account of Politics, Art and Reason Based on Her Psychoanalytic Theory* (New Haven, Conn.: Yale University Press, 1989).

16. Sigmund Freud, *Group Psychology and the Analysis of the Ego*, ed. James Strachey (New York: W. W. Norton, 1959) and *Civilization and Its Discontent*, ed. James Strachey (New York: W. W. Norton, 1961).

17. Melanie Klein, *Envy and Gratitude* (New York: Smirnoff, 1963), 153.

18. The epistemology of ignorance operates, as Sullivan and Tuana write, by "erasing both the achievement of people of color and the atrocities of white people." Sullivan and Tuana, *Race and Epistemologies of Ignorance*, 3. We can also say that epistemological ignorance similarly can characterize the supremacy of the Jewish people in their relations to the Palestinian people.

19. Neve Gordon, *Israel's Occupation* (Berkeley: University of California Press, 2008).

20. Ibid., 13.

21. Ibid., 207.

22. From her clinical experience as a therapist, Lynne Layton acknowledges the defensive process of splitting when approval is given only for performing gender or race "properly." See Lynne Layton, "What Psychoanalysis, Culture and Society Mean to Me," *Mens Sana Monographs* 5 (2007): 1, 147–57.

23. Yannis Stavrakakis, *Lacan and the Political* (New York: Routledge, 1999), 80.

24. In her discussion of Levinas, Butler writes: "[For Levinas] the human is indirectly affirmed in the very disjunction that makes representation impossible, and this disjunction is conveyed in the impossible representation." Yet, she continues, "There is something unrepresentable that we nevertheless seek to represent, and that paradox must be retained in the representation we give." Judith Butler, *Precarious Life: The Power of Mourning and Violence* (London: Verso, 2004), 144. Such is, I believe, the violent paradox created by colonial discourse that speaks on the failure to be loved through practices of exclusion. Sullivan claims that in contrast to the Middle East situation, Puerto Rico's possible acceptance into the United States was because "Puerto Ricans were seen as being receptive to civilizing influences." They, in contrast to the Palestinians, were perceived as cooperative and docile and therefore "hope was not lost," she writes. Sullivan and Tuana, *Race and Epistemologies of Ignorance*, 159.

25. Colonizers, dictators, and, generally, dominant groups in power relations seek approval of their actions through the compliance and loyalty of the other. The "love" of the other also provides for dominant groups reassurance as to their "good" public face and their moral self-image. Ethnic cleansing and genocide occur when a dominant group gives up the desire of the other and seeks total control over the other by mass extermination.

26. Michel Foucault, *Politics, Philosophy, Culture: Interviews and Other Writings, 1977–1984*, trans. Alan Sheridan (New York: Routledge, 1988), 39.

27. Paul Pruyser. "What Splits in 'Splitting'?: A Scrutiny of the Concept of Splitting in Psychoanalysis and Psychiatry," *Bulletin of the Menninger Clinic* 39 (1975): 43.

28. McAfee, born to a Greek mother from Crete, writes that she grew up "hearing about centuries of subjection by the Turks during the Ottoman Empire." One day, she tells, during her student days, she met a Turkish student in a small conference. "Immediately, without any conscious bidding or will, I was filled with dread and horror." This "ancient" fear, she admits, is a common experience of "time collapse" (a concept she borrows from Vamik Volkan), an internalized victimization by minority groups often passing throughout the generations. McAfee, *Democracy*, 2–3.

29. Žižek, *Violence*, 65.

30. See Žižek's similar discussion on freedom. He writes "What is truly traumatic is freedom itself," *Violence*, 196.

31. Jacques Lacan, *The Four Fundamental Concepts of Psycho-Analysis*, trans. Jacques-Alain Miller (New York: W. W. Norton, 1973), 214

4. THE LURE OF PROXIMITY AND THE FEAR OF DEPENDENCY

1. Jacques Lacan, "Desire and the Interpretation of Desire in Hamlet," *Yale French Studies* 55–56 (1977): 11–52.

2. In reference to Auschwitz, Adi Ophir writes: "There is a magic name to the place of a catastrophe. . . . The name presents the whole at once and also its impossible presence. The name says at once: 'Here is that which cannot be said' and 'here this is all that is left to be said.'" Adi Ophir, *Speaking Evil: Towards an Ontology of Morals* (Tel Aviv: Am Oved, 2000), 347. Hebrew.

3. See Marco Belpoliti and Robert Gordon, *The Voice of Memory: Interviews 1961–1987* (Boston: Polity Press, 2001), 185–6.

4. In her 1989 collection of essays *Metaphor and Memory*, Cynthia Ozick published an essay titled "Primo Levi's Suicide Note" in which she argues that the rage he suppressed all his life welled up and caused his suicide. This information was brought to my attention by my friend Janet Burstein in a personal communication.

5. See Ariella Azoulay and Adi Ophir, *This Regime Which Is Not One: Occupation and Democracy between the Sea and the River* (Tel Aviv: Resling, 2008); Neve Gordon, *Israel's Occupation* (Berkeley: University of California Press, 2008).

6. Ernesto Laclau and Chantal Mouffe, *Hegemony and Socialist Strategy: Towards a Radical Democratic Politics* (London: Verso, 2001), 106.

7. For the notion of colonial hybridity that depicts the necessary within power relations, see Homi Bhabha, *The Location of Culture* (New York: Routledge, 1994).

8. Laclau and Mouffe, *Hegemony*, 111.

9. See also Laclau and Mouffe's concept of hegemony; Laclau and Mouffe, *Hegemony*, particularly p. 93.

10. Yannis Stavrakakis, *Lacan and the Political* (New York: Routledge, 1999), 43.

11. On the anthropological self, see Richard A. Shweder and Edmund J. Bourne, "Does the Concept of the Person Vary Cross-Culturally?" in *Culture Theory*, ed. Richard A. Shweder and Robert A, LeVine (Cambridge: Cambridge University Press, 1984), 158–99; Melford Spiro, "Is the Western Conception of the Self 'Peculiar' Within the Context of the World Cultures?" *Ethos* 21 (1993): 107–53. For the psychological self, see Philip Cushman, "The Self in Western Society," in *Constructing the Self, Constructing America: A Cultural History of Psychotherapy* (Reading, Mass.: Addison-Wesley Publishing Company, 1995), 357–87. For the sociological self, see Craig Calhoun, "Social Theory and the Politics of Identity," in *Social Theory and the Politics of Identity* (Oxford, U.K.: Blackwell, 1994), 9–36; Nicolas Rose, "Identity, Genealogy, History," in *Questions of Cultural Identity*, ed. Stuart Hall and Paul du Gay (Thousand Oaks, Calif.: Sage, 1996), 128–50; Ian Hacking, "Making Up People," in *Reconstructing Individualism: Autonomy, Individuality, and the Self in Western Thought*, ed. Thomas H. Heller, Morton Sosna, and David E. Wellbery (Stanford, Calif.: Stanford University Press, 1987), 222–36.

12. Miriam Greenspan, "The Fear of Being Alone: Female Psychology and Women's Work," *Socialist Review* 73 (1984): 93–112.

13. Herbert Marcuse, "Marxism and Feminism," in *City Lights Anthology* (San Francisco: City Lights Books, 1974). See also Sara Ruddick, "Maternal Thinking," *Feminist Studies* 6 (1974): 342–67.

14. There is a lot of talk in medical and psychological journals, as well as in popular advice-books to parents, about how to avoid the problem of dependency in children and how to encourage and develop autonomy and independence.

15. Michel Foucualt, *The Order of Things: An Archaeology of the Human Sciences* (New York: Vintage Books, 1994), xix.

16. Herbert C. Kelman, "The Interdependence of Israeli and Palestinian National Identities: The Role of the Other in Existential Conflict," *Journal of Social Issues* 55 (1999): 3, 589.

17. Ibid., 592.

18. Merlyn B. Brewer, "The Psychology of Prejudice: In-Group Love or Out-Group Hate?" *Journal of Social Issues* 55 (1999): 429–44.

19. Ibid., 436.

20. Ibid., 437.

21. On the paradox of recognition from a psychoanalytic point of view, see Jessica Benjamin, *The Bonds of Love* (New York: Pantheon Books, 1988).

22. I thank Noelle McAfee for pointing this issue out to me.

23. Judith Butler, *Undoing Gender* (New York: Routledge), 44.

24. Ibid., 49.

25. William Connolly, "Discipline, Politics, and Ambiguity," *Political Theory* 11 (1987): 3, 101.

26. Norman Naimark, *Fires of Hatred: Ethnic Cleansing in Twentieth-Century Europe* (Cambridge, Mass.: Harvard University Press, 2001), 24.

27. The Armenian provinces of the Ottoman Empire.

28. Shannon Sullivan, "White Ignorance and Colonial Oppression: Or, Why I Know So Little about Puerto Rico," in *Race and Epistemologies of Ignorance*, ed. Shannon Sullivan and Nancy Tuana (New York: State University of New York Press, 2007), 159.

29. Despite the controversy, I follow here Foucault's thesis: "At the beginning of the seventeenth century . . . thought ceases to move in the element of resemblance. Similitude is no longer the form of knowledge but rather the occasion of error, the danger to which one exposes oneself when one does not examine the obscure region of confusion." Foucault claims that in the nineteenth century knowledge was given an entirely new configuration and went from seeing the empirical domain in terms of kinship, resemblances, and affinities to seeing it in terms of rationalism, measurement, and order. Michel Foucault, *The Order of Things: An Archeology of the Human Sciences* (New York: Vintage Books, 1970), 51–55.

30. Sigmund Freud, "On Narcissism," in *General Psychological Theory*, ed. Philip Rieff (New York: Collier Books, 1963), 118.

31. Such a view can be found in Henry Tajfel and John Turner, "The Social Identity of Inter-Group Behavior," in *Psychology of Inter-Group Relations*, ed. Stephen Worchel and William G. Austin (Chicago: Nelson-Hall, 1986), 24–77, or in Pettigrew F. Thomas, "Intergroup Contact Theory," *Annual Review of Psychology* 49 (1998): 65–85.

32. For example, Muzafer Sherif and Carolyn W. Sherif, "Formation of Out-Group Attitudes and Stereotypes: Experimental Verification," in *Groups in Harmony and Tension: An Integration of Studies on Intergroup Relations* (New York: Octagon Books, 1966), 271–95.

33. Sara Ahmed, *The Cultural Politics of Emotion* (New York: Routledge, 2004), 42–61.

34. When Freud wrote "On Narcissism" in 1915, he had already distinguished between Eros (love) and Thanathos (death).

35. Jacques Derrida, *The Gift of Death* (Chicago: University of Chicago Press, 1995), 64.

36. The Hebraic meaning of *Korban* is both sacrifice and victim.

37. Derrida, *Gift*, 65. This quote also coincides with Lacan's conclusion, "The one you fight is the one you admire the most." The ego ideal, Lacan writes, "is also, according to Hegel's formula which says that coexistence is

impossible, the one you have to kill"; see Jacques Lacan, "Desire and the Interpretation of Desire in Hamlet," *Yale French Studies* 55–56 (1977): 31.

38. Derrida, *Gift*, 64.

39. I am relying here on Michal Ben Naftali's excellent translation of Derrida's *Donner la Mort*, in Orna Ben Naftali and Hannah Naveh, *Trials of Love* (Tel Aviv: Ramot Publication, 2005), 25–42. Hebrew.

40. Derrida, *Gift*, 66

41. Ibid., 85–86.

42. Derrida points out that "the unconditionality of respect for the law also dictates a sacrifice *(Aufopferung)* which is always a sacrifice of the self." In granting death to Isaac, he is inflicting death upon himself. Derrida, *Gift*, 93.

43. Ibid., 91.

44. Ibid., 64.

45. Freud's early views on the life impulse included both love and hate, hatred being perceived as a need for self-preservation, power, and mastery.

46. See Wilhelm Stekel, *The Psychology of Hatred and Cruelty*, vol. 1 (New York: Liveright, 1929).

47. Ibid., 23.

48. See Joseph D. Lichtenberg and Alan Shapard, "Hatred and Its Rewards: A Motivational Systems View," *Psychoanalytic Inquiry* 20 (2000): 274–388; Christopher Bollas, "Loving Hate," *Annual Journal of Psychoanalysis* 12 (1984): 221–37.

49. Glen O. Gabbard, "Hatred and Its Rewards: A Discussion," *Psychoanalytic Inquiry* 20 (2000): 409–19.

50. Bollas "Loving Hate."

51. Lichtenberg and Shapard, "Hatred and Its Rewards."

52. Fred Alford, "Freud and Violence" in *Freud 2000*, ed. Anthony Elliott (Cambridge: Polity Press, 1998), 70.

53. Michael Ignatieff, *The Warrior's Honor: Ethnic War and the Modern Consciousness* (New York: Henry Holt and Company, 1997). Particularly see the chapter on "The Narcissism of Minor Difference," 34–71.

54. Niall Ferguson, *The War of the World: Twentieth-Century Conflict and the Descent of the West* (New York: Penguin Books, 2006); see particularly his section "Inside the 'Folk-Community,'" 245–52.

55. David Duetch, "Anti-Semitism and Intimacy in Goebbels Writings," paper under review.

56. Jacques Derrida, "Differance," in *Speech and Phenomenon* (Evanston, Ill.: Northwestern University Press, 1973), 129.

57. Alain Badiou, *Polemics* (London: Verso, 2011), 185.

58. See Slavoj Žižek's commentary on the difference between Nazism and Stalinism in his answer to his critiques in "Some concluding notes on violence, ideology, and communist culture," *Subjectivity* 3 (2010): 101–16.

59. Žižek, *Subjectivity*, 130.

60. By "surface differences" I do not mean to say that, in contrast, there are deep differences that are veiled or hidden. I am saying that stressed group differences, no matter how deep or superficial one conceives them to be, are conscious representations that unconsciously deny needs and desire.

61. A fascinating case of colonial relations of proximity in a space of unequal relations of dependency resulting in shared panic is suggested by Homi Bhabha retelling the events that occurred between 1850 and 1860 and that led to the Indian mutiny. Bhabha, *Location of Culture*, and also "In Spirit of Calm Violence," in *After Colonialism: Imperial Histories and Postcolonial Displacements*, ed. Parakash Gyan (Princeton, N.J.: Princeton University Press, 1995), 326–43. Another example of emotional dependency within social and political power relations see J.M. Barbalet, *Emotion, Social Theory and Social Structure* (Cambridge: Cambridge University Press, 2001), 149–69.

62. I do not mean here a natural or cultural resemblance, but one that is based on our imagination of things; take, for example, proximity as a sign of similarity. See Foucault's discussion of "Representing," in *Order of Things*, 46–77.

63. Yuval Portugali, *Implicate Relations: Society and Space in the Israeli Palestinian Conflict* (Tel Aviv: Hakibbutz Hameuchad, 1996), 11. Hebrew.

64. Ariella Azoulay and Adi Ophir, *This Regime Which Is Not One: Occupation and Democracy between the Sea and the River* (Tel Aviv: Resling, 2008). Hebrew.

65. Gabriel Piterberg, *The Return of Zionism: Myths, Politics and Scholarship in Israel* (London: Verso, 2008), 209.

66. Ibid., 213.

67. Edward Said in an interview published to *Haaretz* newspaper, 18 August 2000.

68. Foucault, *Order of Things*, 145.

69. Sara Ahmed, *The Cultural Politics of Emotions* (New York: Routledge, 2004).

70. Many studies on twentieth-century regional conflicts and civil wars that have included genocide and ethnic cleansing show that hatred erupts suddenly between intimate, close neighbors. See, for example, Naimark, *Fires of Hatred*.

71. Azoulay and Ophir, *This Regime*; Gordon, *Israel's Occupation*.

72. Judith Butler, *The Psychic Life of Power: Theories in Subjection* (Palo Alto, Calif.: Stanford University Press, 1997), 8.

73. See Robert S. Robins and Jerrold M. Post, who like Ahmed also conclude that "ironically those groups from which we most passionately distinguish ourselves are those to which we are most closely bound," in *Political Paranoia: The Psychopolitics of Hatred* (New Haven, Conn.: Yale University Press, 1997), 92.

74. Gordon, *Israel's Occupation*.

75. Ahmed, *Cultural Politics*.

76. Michael Hardt and Antonio Negri, *Multitude: War and Democracy in the Age of Empire* (New York: Penguin Press, 2004).

77. In *Multitude*, Hardt and Negri claim that, in the new era (the passage from modernity to postmodernism), war has become a general condition. Wars today are no longer isolated, distinct, and unique. Wars have become global, permanent, and the continuation of politics by other means.

5. FROM JUSTICE TO POLITICAL FRIENDSHIP

1. Jacques Derrida, *The Politics of Friendship* (London: Verso, 1994), 235.

2. Ibid., 236.

3. Formal justice is defined as that which is negotiated by leaders yet not necessarily accepted by most members of society. See Daniel Bar-Tal and Gemma H. Bennink, "The Nature of Reconciliation as an Outcome and as a Process," in *From Conflict Resolution to Reconciliation*, ed. Yaacov Bar-Siman-Tov (Oxford: Oxford University Press, 2004), 12.

4. For further elaboration of "overlapping consensus" and justice as fairness, see John Rawls, "The Domain of the Political and Overlapping Consensus," *New York University Law Review* 64 (1989): 233–55.

5. Ronald Fisher, "Social-Psychological Processes in Interactive Conflict Analysis and Reconciliation," in *Reconciliation, Justice and Coexistence*, ed. Muhamed Abu-Nimer (New York: Lexington Books, 2001), 54.

6. Bar-Siman-Tov, *From Conflict Resolution*.

7. Bar-Tal and Bennink, "The Nature of Reconciliation as an Outcome and as a Process," in Bar-Siman-Tov, *From Conflict Resolution*, 11–38.

8. Bar-Siman-Tov, *From Conflict Resolution*, 4.

9. Paul Ahluwalia, "Towards (Re)Conciliation: The Post-Colonial Economy of Giving," *Social Identities* 6, no. 1 (2000): 39.

10. According to the liberal principles of fairness on which the court based its decision, it was claimed that emotions must and should be considered if they do not exceed certain reasonableness that the court called "measureliness."

11. For a fruitful discussion of political friendship in ancient Greek culture, see Danielle S. Allen, *Talking to Strangers: Anxieties of Citizenship since Brown v. Board of Education* (Chicago: University of Chicago Press, 2004).

12. Ahluwalia develops an analysis of the postcolonial economy of giving in the service of reconciliation. Giving, like "a gift that does not entail a direct return," he claims, "seeks to break down the cycles of revenge." Giving a gift, according to Bataille, signifies an acquisition of power by the very fact of losing it. See Ahluwalia, "Towards (Re)Conciliation," 38–40; Georges Bataille, "The Gift of Rivalry: 'Potlatch'" in *The Bataille Reader*, ed. Fred Botting and Scott Wilson (New York: Wiley-Blackwell, 1997), 201–36.

13. Yehudith Auerbach, "The Role of Forgiveness in Reconciliation," in Bar-Siman-Tov, *From Conflict Resolution*, 153.

14. Derrida defines the Abrahamic tradition as that which brings together Judaism, Christianity, and Islam. Jacques Derrida, *On Cosmopolitanism and Forgiveness* (New York: Routledge, 2001).

15. Ibid., 32.

16. Ibid., 32.

17. Ibid., 34.

18. Ibid., 48–49.

19. The decision in 1964 France that "crimes against humanity were to remain imprescriptible" is an example of one that is simultaneously juridical and transcendent. It signals, writes Derrida, the forgiveness of the unforgivable and in general "of a certain beyond of the law (beyond all historical determination of the law)"; Derrida, *On Cosmopolitanism*, 52.

20. Ibid., 53.

21. Ibid., 54–55.

22. Ibid., 49.

23. Allen, *Talking to Strangers*.

24. See the discussion on Butler's concept of the political unconscious in Chapter 1, particularly her theorization of the absent other who "was never loved and never lost."

25. Allen, *Talking to Strangers*, 119.

26. Ibid., 134.

27. Ibid., 130.

28. Ibid., 154.

29. Allen asks: "And isn't brotherhood vague, touchy-feel, and also, as the French revolutionary proved, dangerous?" Allen, *Talking to Strangers*, 118.

30. Derrida, *On Cosmopolitanism* .

31. George L. Mosse, *Fallen Soldiers: Reshaping the Memory of World Wars* (Oxford: Oxford University Press, 1990). See also Mosse, *The Image of Man: The Creation of Modern Masculinity* (Oxford: Oxford University Press, 1996).

32. Danny Kaplan and Niza Yanay, "Fraternal Friendship and Commemorative Desire," *Social Analysis* 50 (2006): 127–46.

33. Ibid., 139.

34. Derrida, *The Politics of Friendship*, 302.

35. See David Halperin, *One Hundred Years of Homosexuality, and Other Essays on Greek Love* (New York: Routledge, 1990).

36. Ibid., 142.

37. Another is the question of numbers. How many friends are there? The question of numbers is brought up in relation to Aristotle's cry "Oh, my friends, there is no friend." Derrida, *Politics*.

38. Ibid., 105.

39. Ibid., 72.

40. Derrida goes into a lengthy discussion to point out the contradictions and aporias of each type of friendship when translated into a democratic notion of politics.

41. Derrida, *Politics*, 205.

42. In fact, Derrida writes "*only* in friendship." But in order to be more accurately in accord with his conclusions, I have chosen to use "always," which I believe is a more adequate idea in relation to his later arguments. Derrida, *Politics*, 224.

43. Simon Critchley reminds us that for Blanchot and Derrida *philia* is *necrophilia*. "One is only a friend of that which is going to die," he writes. Saying adieu to a friend, dead or living, is to acknowledge the other's mortality. See Simon Critchley, "The Other's Decision in Me: (What Are the Politics of Friendship?)," *European Journal of Social Theory* 1 (19981): 2, 259–79.

44. Derrida, *Politics*, 254.

45. Ibid., 254.

46. Critchley, " Other's Decision," 263.

47. By contrast, Israeli leaders have often declared that they are ready to meet with any Arab leader, but their declarations have been rhetorical and unreliable. For example, in 1955 Ben-Gurion claimed that he was willing to meet with the Egyptian president to talk peace as soon as possible and without preconditions, but then by the end of the day he ordered an attack on Egypt in which fifty Egyptian soldiers were killed and forty-nine were taken as hostages. That battle, said Nasser, the Egyptian president, doubtlessly proved that Ben-Gurion was not sincere in his declarations. See A. Israeli (or/and Machover), *Peace, Peace and No Peace: Israel and the Arab Countries 1948–1961* (Hertzelia: P.O.B. 3050, 1999).

48. Victims do not have the luxury of losing the power they gain by withholding the response of friendship.

49. Critchley notes that for Derrida the term "messianic" is related to a whole linguistic chain—*aimance*, justice, democracy to come, or unconditioned hospitality—with a similar, but not identical, function. He adds that this term, however, does not imply that Derrida avoids concrete political questions. Critchley, 265, 274.

50. Adi Ophir, *The Order of Evils: Towards an Ontology of Morals* (New York: Zone Books, 2005), 317.

51. Ophir defines presence as "a relation, a relation between what-is-present and someone-who-is-presented with what-is-present." Therefore, he continues, "presence, unlike existence, cannot be the predicate of an object without splitting the object itself or multiplying it into what is present and who is pre-

sented with it, or, that is, without attributing it to a witness." Ophir, *Order of Evils*, 170. For further reading on Ophir's notions of the present and presence, see also 170–210.

52. Although I am not making a gendered argument here, and although I do not think that women more than men must take the responsibility for preventing harm and suffering, it is hard not to think about the vast amount of feminist literature, particularly during the 1980s, that emphasized, following Nancy Chodorow and Carol Gilligan, women's ethic of care and responsibility for others grounded in women's experience of nurturance as mothers, associating between the principle of care and responsibility and the practice of peace and sisterhood.

53. Judith Butler, *Giving an Account of Oneself* (New York: Fordham University Press, 2005), 84.

54. The law works under the assumption that punishment for crimes and injustice will serve to prevent harm and suffering in the future, but the law's preventive force (if any) is not identical to the law itself.

55. Ophir notes that the opposite of presence is absence rather than disappearance, which signifies a certain invisibility but not absence.

56. In *Giving an Account of Oneself*, Butler speaks of the difficulty to even narrate such dependency in which the "I" is "given over" to the other, 82.

57. Butler raises this possibility in her discussion of Laplanche. Butler, *Giving an Account*, 84.

58. Here I differ from Schmitt's concept of the political which separates between the enemy and friend as the limiting boundary of the political.

59. Helen Cooper and Mark Landler, "White House Pivots in Mideast Peace Bid," *New York Times*, 23 September 2009, sec. A1, p. 7.

60. Ophir writes, "For the one who remains indifferent, who refuses to turn another's problem into his problem, the subjectivity of the victim of a wrong is as unrecognized as the evil that turns her into a victim." Ophir, *Order of Evils*, 281. He gives a moving example of a sick child whose immediate problems concern his parents, but when "the family reaches the army checkpoint with the child, in hope of making it to the hospital on the other side of the blockade . . . the soldiers' problem is the car that broke the curfew and not the awful condition of the child," 375. Preventing such indifference to suffering is the face of friendship.

61. Alan Vanier, "Fear, Paranoia and Politics," unpublished lecture translated from the French by Joan Monahan.

62. Scott Shane, "Rethinking What to Fear," *New York Times*, 27 September 2009, p. 1.

63. Julia Kristeva, *Strangers to Ourselves* (New York: Columbia University Press, 1991), 170.

64. Mahmud Darwish, *Bed of a Stranger: Poems* (Tel Aviv: Babel Press, 2000). The citations are my own translation from Hebrew. Jacques Ranciere express a similar idea of "being together" in "being apart" offered by relations of artistic mediation. Jacque Ranciere, *The Emancipated Spectator* (London: Verso, 2009).

65. For a similar analysis in a different context, see my article (with Nitza Berkovitch) "Gender Imago: Searching for New Feminist Methodologies," *Cultural Studies/Critical Methodologies* 6 (2009): 2, 193–216.

66. See also Jacqueline Rose, *The Last Resistance* (London: Verso, 2007).

67. Ahluwalia, "Towards (Re)Conciliation," 29–48.

68. In an article on the autonomy of the political, Shenhav criticizes the Schmittian definition of the political as being total, limiting, and narrow, contending that Schmitt's focus on the absolute distinction between friend and enemy fixates the political to the frame of the nation-state and does not allow other forms of criticism of governmentality and bio-power. See Yehuda Shenhav, "On the Auto-nomous of the Political," *Theory and Criticism* 34 (2009): 181–90. Hebrew. I agree with Shenhav only partially. It is true that traces of the political infiltrate and reconstruct relations between other systems besides the nation-state, and even more so the political relations between groups and subjects. Yet the nodal point of the political remains, perhaps not always directly and not always sharply delineated, the distinction between the friend and enemy in different ways, through different representations and meanings.